Jonas Cramby is a freelance writer, restaurant critic and columnist.
His highly praised cookbook *Tex-Mex from Scratch* was published in
2012 and the equally celebrated *Texas BBQ* in 2013. The books have
been translated into six languages. He lives with his family in Sweden.

THE ULTIMATE
SANDWICH

Jonas Cramby

Photography: Roland Persson

PAVILION

Contents

I hate sandwiches...

I ALSO LOVE THEM. It happened like this. Growing up I had a constantly ongoing conflict with my family, which in some way might be the basis for my ambivalent attitude towards sandwiches today. Every time my parents bought fresh bread, they would hide it away in the cupboard, as we 'must finish off the old first'. Perhaps this sounded clever in theory, but the consequence was that when the old bread was finally finished, the new one had also turned dry and boring – resulting in us never being able to eat fresh, tasty bread. It was a vicious circle of bread (a croissant?) that eventually made me develop a hatred of sandwiches. I thought they were dry and boring and something that one would force oneself to get through, like the culinary answer to a vocabulary test.

Of course, my prejudices towards sandwiches didn't improve when I moved away from home, when sandwiches became loveless fast food that I'd scoff down in between two meetings. I ate them from a plastic wrap, stuffed with a lump of mayo-drenched filling and a wilted lettuce leaf that smelled like it does in between your toes. At cafés it was almost worse; there you'd get served tough and dry ciabatta bread with an ice-cold lump of margarine (not even spread out), rolled-up slices of pre-cut cheese and either a quarter of a standard tomato or a whole small one – and then, just to make sure no one gets offended, an inedible stalk of parsley on the top. If there's just one detail that really says something about our attitude towards lunch sandwiches, it's those quarters of vegetables that we put on them – can we not even be bothered to slice our peppers and tomatoes properly? Don't we think it's worth another thirty seconds of preparation time to achieve a more even distribution of vegetables? I can almost get offended when I am served a sandwich like that. It's like it's saying: 'I hate my job and despise you for eating here.'

Then the low-carb diet came along, and bread was suddenly the great white Satan. TV dieticians dramatically threw sandwiches in the bin and exclaimed: 'I don't call them slices of bread, I call them slices of dead'. When we finally realised that these people were actually raving mad, the next big blow hit the sandwich culture: the sourdough trend.

Don't get me wrong; I love sourdough bread. I think it's beautiful, tasty and a nice little hobby to have. But whereas sandwiches are all about the whole, most of the rustic sourdough breads are just 'me, me, me' all the time. It's almost impossible to eat them with anything else than a slice of cheese or a dollop of marmalade. They have big holes in them so you're pretty much buttering the chopping board rather than the bread; they tear your palate open and are so compact and chewy that whichever filling you throw in them is quickly forced into submission. The sourdough loaf is, simply put, a diva, an individualist, while the bread required for a really good sandwich has to be a team player.

Because, as I said, a sandwich is all about the whole – about neither the bread nor the filling nor the condiment taking over. They are a perfect example of solidarity. When you eat food from a plate you can combine together a good mouthful yourself, while in a sandwich you'll need an absolutely perfect balance between flavour and texture from the very beginning in each individual bite. And this might be the reason for our shabby sandwich culture: that we underrate the sandwich. We think we can just throw one together with the fridge door still open, when in fact, making a great sandwich is something of an art form.

The first time I realised what a sandwich could really mean was at the seafront in Nice on the French Riviera. I was probably six or seven years old and my parents had bought me a caprese baguette from one of the small sandwich shops that were everywhere. When I took the first crispy bite and felt how the soft, freshly made mozzarella counterbalanced the acidity and sweetness of the sun-blushed tomatoes and the

bite of the black pepper, it was as though a veil had lifted from my vision, and at once I realised that the world was so much bigger and more beautiful than just a dry flatbread with spreadable liver pâté. It was as if that caprese sandwich said: 'Hey, you, I've made a sandwich that I'm very proud of – fancy a bite?'

Since then, I've mostly searched for, and found, my sandwich highs when I've been away from my home in Sweden. Because almost everywhere you end up in the world there are varieties of the portable, cheap – but above all tasty – sandwich. To eat smørrebrød and get daytime boozy in Copenhagen is one of the finer things in life. So is eating a pastrami on rye at a deli in New York, a croque at a café in Paris or a bao from a street stall in Taiwan. And despite the fact we might not have much of a lunch sandwich culture to speak of in Sweden, yet we are excellent when it comes to good-quality ingredients and classic food crafts like making sausage, cheese and pâtés. And perhaps it's from there we'll have to move on if we want to get better at making sandwiches. Because that's what we want, right?

Now, I don't want to overstate the importance of the sandwich, but there is almost an existential dimension in a really well composed sandwich. To dig your teeth into one of those is what makes you start asking questions like: Why do we so often neglect the things that actually feed us? Why can we spend an enormous effort, and vast sums of money, on Saturday dinner, but still accept plastic-wrapped mayonnaise bombs for weekday lunch? Why do we save the fresh bread in order to finish off the old one first? When the answer really is, as the musician Warren Zevon said on his deathbed: 'Enjoy every sandwich'.

– Jonas Cramby

LAYERS OF CURIOSITY

THIS COOKBOOK IS meant to be layered, meaning that you can choose either to make your sandwiches completely from scratch or buy all the ingredients in a shop and then assemble them at home – or do something in between.

Take, for example, this picture. The bacon, you can smoke yourself or buy. The bread, you can bake or pick up from an artisan baker. The same for the mustard, the mayo, the butter – yes, even the chopping board. Where you draw your line on what's worth doing is, of course, up to you.

But before you put your jacket on and go off to nearest deli, consider the following. Quite apart from the fact that it's a whole lot tastier to prepare the food yourself, it's also cheaper, it's more sustainable and makes you more aware of possible additives – and gives you the chance to avoid them. It makes people that you love happy, and then there's that simple joy of standing by the work surface, humming, and actually creating stuff with your own hands. Then, let's not forget, an interest in food is, to a great extent, also about curiosity. Perhaps you won't make your own mozzarella every time you make home-made pizza for a Friday night in, but perhaps you'll want to try it out at least once, so that you know how it works.

Yet people who weren't blessed with this kind of curiosity will never understand why you're doing this. 'How can you be bothered?' they'll ask, and some might even get provoked and perhaps call you a nerd or a foodie, or claim that your interest for food only stems from that ambiguous idea of status – as if that would be the only drive that exists. They will take your hobbies as a personal offence. But before you get offended at their attitude, think about how boring it must be to live that way; to regard food, which at its very core actually is life, as something that's not worth doing properly.

So instead of becoming angry, I think you should pat these people on the back and say, with just a hint of condescension: 'It will all be okay, mate'. That you take the moral high-ground doesn't mean, of course, that you ought to make them any of the sandwiches in this book. They can make their own damn sandwich.

Pain
de MIE

This French classic is the original sandwich bread and a predecessor to supermarket additive-packed batch loaves — just tremendously tastier, healthier and certainly better looking. The butter will add a bit of a brioche taste to the bread, which has a beautiful crust and perfect crunch when toasted. Bake a batch and keep it pre-sliced in the freezer, like a turbo-fuelled breakfast toast, or use it as a base for one of this chapter's sandwiches.

Pain de mie

The French word 'mie' means crumb, and that's exactly what this bread is about. To achieve a perfectly square form, minimal amount of crust as well as the right compact but soft, buttery crumb, the pan de mie is often baked in a special tin with a sliding lid, but you can just as well use a standard tin with a chopping board as a weight on top.

Makes a 900g/2lb loaf

250 ml/9fl oz/generous 1 cup tepid water
250ml/9fl oz/generous 1 cup whole milk
625g/1lb 6oz/5 cups strong white bread flour, plus extra to dust
2½ tsp sea salt
1 tbsp clear honey
100 g/3½ oz butter
a little oil for greasing

1. Mix together the yeast and water directly in the dough mixer bowl. Add the milk, flour, salt and honey and run the machine for 2 minutes. Leave to rest for 2 minutes, then run for a further 2 minutes. If you are kneading by hand, double all the kneading times.

2. Put the butter in between two layers of clingfilm and start beating it with a rolling pin like a mad person. Continue until the butter is soft but hasn't started to melt. With the machine running, add small dollops of butter at a time to the dough through the feed tube until all butter is kneaded into the dough. Turn the dough out onto a floured worktop.

3. The dough should be a little sticky to touch but still mouldable. Fold it in half, then turn it 180 degrees and fold again. Fold a third time. Shape into a large bun, put in a lightly oiled bowl and cover with clingfilm. Leave to rise at room temperature until almost tripled in size, about 3 hours.

4. Take out the dough and place onto a floured worktop. Knock it back and fold on the centre. Repeat three times in total. Place back into the bowl, cover with clingfilm and leave to rise for another 2 hours, or until doubled in size.

5. This is the moment when it's good to have a bit of flair. Confidently and feeling a bit superior, as if you were a baker, take the dough out of the bowl, fold lengthways and mould into a loaf shape. Place the vaguely loaf-shaped dough, seam downwards, into a pan de mie tin or other rectangular bread tin and press out gently with floured hands. Cover with clingfilm. Leave to prove until the dough has reached 1cm/½in below the edge. It will take about 1 hour.

6. Preheat the oven to 220°C/425°F/gas 7. When the dough is ready, slide the lid over the tin. If you are using a standard tin, cover with a heat-resistant chopping board or baking sheet with a weight on top. Bake in the centre of the oven for 40 minutes. Remove the bread from the tin and leave to cool completely before slicing. Prepare to be amazed by the perfectly square shape.

THE SANDWICH LOVER'S GUIDE TO BAKING EQUIPMENT

New England-style hot dog bun pan. For the perfectly shaped hot dog bun. Can be replaced by a standard deep baking tray.

Baguette tray. Keeps the shape of the dough, plus the tiny little holes mean the underside gets crispy.

Round tray for focaccia and muffuletta. Can be replaced by a standard deep tin.

Cutter. Round shape for cutting out biscuits, for example. Can be replaced by a glass.

Dough mixer. Indispensable for all of us who don't see the sense in kneading. It can be a table mixer with a dough hook or a food processor or, of course, be replaced by muscle strength.

Pan de mie tin with sliding lid. Can be replaced by a rectangular tin with a heat-resistant chopping board, or with a baking sheet with a suitable weight on top.

Grilled cheese with tomato soup

In its simplest form, the toasted cheese sandwich with tomato soup makes a tasty weekday meal. Stovetop grill the sandwich and it is transformed into a feast worthy of a king or queen. Freshly shaved truffle will make the sandwich reach sublime heights – but if it's not the season for it, or you're a stingy one, skip it. It will be tasty anyway. Use a slightly milder cheese if you make the sandwich with truffle.

Serves 4

FOR THE SOUP

4 slices of smoked bacon (see page 96)
4 garlic cloves, chopped
1 brown onion, chopped
1 carrot, chopped
50g/1¾oz butter
3 tbsp tomato purée
1 tbsp plain flour
1 litre/1¾ pints/4⅓ cups chicken stock
2 fresh thyme sprigs
1 bay leaf
400g/14oz can of whole plum tomatoes
salt and freshly ground black pepper

FOR THE SANDWICH

8 slices of Pain de Mie, about 2 cm/¾in thick (see page 12)
300g/11oz Gruyère or Comté cheese, grated
1 small fresh black truffle (optional)
softened butter
sea salt

1. Start by making the soup. Put the pork in a saucepan over a medium heat and fry until crisp. Turn the heat up one level, add the butter and the chopped vegetables and fry until the vegetables have softened. Add tomato purée and flour and fry, stirring, for another minute. Add the stock, thyme, bay leaf and tomatoes. Lower the heat and leave to simmer for 30 minutes.

2. Take out the bay leaf and thyme and blend the soup until smooth, then pour it back into the pan. Season to taste with salt and pepper. Keep it warm over a low heat until it's time to eat, or leave to cool, then put it in the fridge and heat up later.

3. Finally it's time to make the sandwiches! Butter one side of the bread slices with a thin, thin layer of soft butter and place half of them with the buttered-side down in a frying pan. Add the grated cheese and shaved truffle, if using. Sprinkle with salt and place the other slice of bread on top. Press down gently with a broad spatula or a grill press. The key to a really good grilled cheese is to leave the bread to brown in peace so that the cheese gets a chance to melt properly. Cook each side for 8–10 minutes, making sure the hob is on a medium heat.

4. When the bottom slice has turned a nice brown colour, flip the sandwiches over carefully and cook for another 8–10 minutes. Take out the sandwiches, cut into triangles and serve with the tomato soup. Whether or not you dip the sandwich is, of course, completely up to you, but I would never miss out on a dipping opportunity – are you mad?!

THE ANATOMY OF A PERFECT GRILLED CHEESE

1. Melted, yummy cheese.

2. Some kind of amalgamation of bread and cheese, called 'breese'. Love the breese.

3. Warm, soft bread.

4. Crispy, buttery crust.

Croque madame

Simone de Beauvoir was wrong: woman isn't the second sex. Woman is the first, at least when it comes to grilled sandwiches. To my mind, everything becomes tastier if you put a fried egg on top. This applies especially to the French bistro classic croque monsieur, which is transformed into the, in every sense, superior croque madame just by adding one of those.

Serves 4

8 slices of Pan de Mie, about 1½ cm/3/8in thick (see page 12)
Dijon mustard
12 thin slices of boiled ham
200g/7oz Gruyère or Comté cheese, grated
4 eggs
1–2 tbsp finely chopped chives
green or tomato salad to serve

FOR THE MORNAY SAUCE

½ tbsp butter
1½ tbsp plain flour
300ml/10½fl oz/generous 1¼ cups whole milk
a pinch of grated nutmeg
4 tbsp grated Parmesan cheese
100g/3½oz Gruyère or Comté cheese, grated
salt and freshly ground black pepper

1. Preheat the oven to 200°C/400°F/gas 6 and then get cracking with the mornay sauce. A mornay sauce is a béchamel sauce with cheese, so don't be scared, just start as per usual and melt the butter in a saucepan over a medium heat. Whisk in the flour, pour over the milk and add a pinch of nutmeg. Bring to the boil, stirring, until you get a creamy sauce. Add the Parmesan and grated Gruyère. Leave the cheese to melt while stirring. Season to taste with salt and pepper.

2. Toast the bread slices, then spread them with mustard. Place 3 thin slices of ham on each of 4 of the slices and top with about half of the cheese, then cover with the remaining bread slices (mustard-side down, of course). Pour mornay sauce over the whole thing and sprinkle with the remaining Gruyère.

3. Bake in the centre of the oven for 5–8 minutes, or until all the cheese has melted and the mornay sauce has started to bubble and turn a nice colour.

4. Meanwhile, fry the eggs. Serve the sandwiches finished off with a fried egg and garnished with some chives. Serve with a simple green or tomato salad and an ice cold Kronenburg in one of those silly little bottles. Close your eyes and relive that first, magical InterRail trip you made when you bought a leather pouch for your lighter, got a UV tattoo around your belly button and pulled/got into a fight with a tout for the Le Banana boat disco in Juan-les-Pins.

OTHER FAMOUS CROQUES

CROQUE MONSIEUR
Like a madame but without the egg.

CROQUE PROVENÇAL
With tomato.

CROQUE NORVÉGIEN
With smoked salmon instead of ham.

CROQUE TARTIFLETTE
With thinly sliced potato and Reblochon cheese.

CROQUE SEÑOR
With hot tomato salsa.

CROQUE HAWAIIAN
With a slice of pineapple.

BLT (BACON LETTUCE TOMATO)

The simpler the sandwich, the better-quality ingredients you'll need. But what do you do if you fancy a humble BLT and have some really good bacon in but it's not one of the few weeks a year when local tomatoes actually taste of something? Well, you roast cherry tomatoes in the oven to maximise the tomato flavour and complement them with fresh tomatoes to raise the freshness level a notch.

Makes 4 sandwiches

8 slices of Pain de Mie, about 1.5cm/⅝in thick (see page 12)
12 cherry tomatoes, halved and deseeded
2 tbsp olive oil
6 garlic cloves, unpeeled
150ml/5fl oz/scant ⅔ cup Mayonnaise (see page 32)
a pot of fresh basil
300g/10½oz finest-quality bacon (see page 96)
4 iceberg lettuce leaves
4 ripe tomatoes, sliced
salt and freshly ground black pepper

1. Preheat the oven to 150°C/300°C/gas 2. Put the cherry tomatoes in a baking tray, drizzle over the olive oil and season with salt and pepper. Oh, and throw in the garlic for the mayo while you're at it, too. Peel and everything still on. Roast for about 45 minutes, or until they get crinkly and a little caramelised.

2. When tomato and garlic look nice, take them out of the oven. Squeeze the now squashy garlic out of the peel and mix together with the mayo. Roughly tear up the basil leaves and stir them in, too.

3. Fry the bacon in a hot pan and leave drain on a piece of kitchen paper. Soak the lettuce in iced water to maximise crunch and freshness.

4. Now it's time to assemble the sandwich. Do this by browning the bread slices on one side in a non-stick pan. The toasted side should be turned towards the inside of the sandwich to give some crunch and to provide a barrier for the mayo, with the soft side facing out so that it is soft and smooth in the mouth. It's these details that are important for us sandwich lovers. Spread the basil mayo on the toasted side of the bread, add the lettuce, bacon and both baked and sliced fresh tomatoes. Finish off by placing another mayo-prepped bread slice on top, cut into triangles and dig in.

BACON SARNIE

The British bacon sarnie and is, at its best, both a subtle and sublime creation (and at its worst, pretty nasty, actually). This is how to make a good version.

MAKES 4 SANDWICHES

4 slices of Pain de Mie, about 1.5cm/⅝in thick (see page 12)
300g/11oz finest-quality bacon (see page 96)
fridge-cold butter

Fry the bacon until crispy, then leave to drain on a piece of kitchen paper. Butter the bread with the fridge-cold butter. The idea with this is partly that it should be as difficult as possible to spread, so that you're forced to use an embarrassingly large amount, partly that the cold butter should contrast with the warm filling – just like the soft, untoasted bread should stand as a contrast to the crispy bacon.

Club sandwich

The old room-service favourite, the club sandwich is one of those sandwiches that people feel they have to reinvent all the time. But sometimes the classic is actually the best, so here follows the exact recipe for how the original club sandwich was served at the gambling club in Saratoga Springs where it was invented at some point at the end of the nineteenth century. Cocktail sticks with tassels are, as I'm sure you can understand, a must.

Makes 4 sandwiches

12 slices of Pain de Mie, about 1cm/½in thick (see page 12)
8 slices of finest-quality bacon (see page 96)
4 tomatoes, sliced
4 iceberg lettuce leaves
Mayonnaise (see page 32)
16 cocktail sticks
salt and freshly ground black pepper

FOR THE TURKEY

350g/12oz turkey breast
1 brown onion, sliced
1 lemon, sliced
6 garlic cloves
1 litre/1¾ pints/4⅓ cups water
3 tbsp salt
1½ tbsp granulated sugar
a bunch of fresh tarragon
a bunch of fresh parsley
1 bay leaf
1 tbsp whole black peppercorns

1. One day ahead you'll need to leave the turkey to soak in a salt brine so that it gets juicy and tasty when cooked. Put all the turkey ingredients (except the turkey) into a pan and bring to the boil, then leave to cool. Pour the salt brine over the turkey, making sure it's covered, cover with clingfilm and put in the fridge.

2. The next day, take out the turkey from the brine and leave to dry for 1 hour in the fridge.

3. Pre-heat the oven to 230°C/450°F/gas 8 and roast the turkey in the centre of the oven until the juices run clear when the thickest part is pierced with a skewer. Take it out, leave to rest until cool and then slice thinly.

4. Meanwhile, fry the bacon until crispy in a frying pan, or cook it in the oven. A short dip into iced water will make the lettuce even crispier.

5. Assemble the sandwich by toasting 3 slices of bread per person. Spread mayo on the bottom slice and place salad and turkey on top. Add the centre bread slice, crispy bacon and sliced tomato. Sprinkle with salt and pepper. Spread mayo on the bottom side of the last slice of bread and press on top. Pierce with four cocktail sticks and slice the sandwich diagonally so you end up with four perfect triangles with one cocktail stick in each. Serve with fries and beer while lying in bed watching TV.

OTHER FAMOUS CLUB SANDWICHES

CHICKEN CLUB
Replace the turkey with chicken.

ROAST BEEF CLUB
Replace the turkey with thinly sliced roast beef.

BREAKFAST CLUB
Replace the turkey with a fried egg.

AVOCADO CLUB
Add thinly sliced avocado.

LOBSTER CLUB
Replace the turkey with chopped freshly boiled lobster tossed in some mayo, a couple of drops lemon juice and a thinly sliced avocado.

21

'Nutella' spread sandwich

Having hazelnut chocolate on your sandwich is for us porridge-eating inhabitants of the North totally depraved, a little bit like sprinkling cocaine on your breakfast cereal. We do, however, have a little rule in my family that does allow you eat sweet things for breakfast — but only if you've made it yourself. A loophole that I think you ought to introduce as well, because a mouthful of really good toasted bread with chocolate-nut spread and a sprinkle of salt flakes is actually quite hard to beat, right?

Makes 4 slices

4 slices of Pain de Mie (see page 12)
butter
flake salt

FOR THE NUT AND CHOCOLATE SPREAD

200g/7oz/1½ cups hazelnuts
100g/3½oz dark chocolate (at least 70% cocoa solids)
400g/14oz can of condensed milk
1 tbsp milk (you might not need this)

1. Start by making the spread. Toast the nuts in a warm, dry frying pan until the aroma rises from the pan. If you want you can you can remove those skins. If not, don't bother.

2. Start blending the nuts. This will take a lot longer than you can imagine, perhaps half an hour in total. First, they will look like they're chopped (image 1), which they are, but then you have to keep going. After 5–10 minutes they will transform into a kind of dough (image 2), and then it's important that you continue for a little longer. Don't give up now. Fight. Just when you think that there's something wrong with your nuts, something will happen. That dough suddenly turns into a creamy nut butter (image 3).

3. Melt the chocolate in the condensed milk in a saucepan on the hob and then mix it with the nut butter until a lovely home-made chocolate and nut spread appears. If the paste is too thick, stir in some milk.

4. Toast the bread, spread with butter and your wonderful spread, then finish off with a few salt flakes.

Peanut butter and jelly sandwich

Research has shown that when the average American has finished high school, he or she has already managed to eat 2,500 peanut butter and jelly sandwiches. And it's no surprise, since the pb&j has got that lovely mix of sweet and salty, creamy and crispy that you get mad cravings for when you come home from swimming practice with icicles in your hair and sit down to watch some cartoons.

Makes 4 sandwiches

8 slices of Pain de Mie
  (see page 12)
butter

FOR THE PEANUT AND ALMOND BUTTER

240g/8½oz/1½ cups
  salted peanuts
150g/5oz/1 cup almonds
2 tsp clear honey
1 tsp salt

FOR THE GRAPE JELLY

1kg/2lb 4oz red grapes,
  the deeper the colour
  the better
100ml/3½fl oz/
  scant ½ cup water
1 lemon
450g/1lb/2 cups jam
  sugar with pectin

1. Start by making the peanut and almond butter. Preheat the oven to 150°C/300°C/gas 2. Slow roasting is the key to a flavourful peanut butter, so spread the nuts and the almonds out on an oven tray and roast on the centre shelf for 20 minutes or until they start to colour – making sure they don't burn. Stir occasionally. Taste. Once ready, put them in a blender with the honey and salt and mix. If you like your peanut butter crunchy, take out 2 tbsp of nuts when they look suitably crushed. Then keep on blending the rest until, as if by pure magic, they turn from nut dust into a creamy butter. It will take at least a quarter of an hour. Then stir the chunky peanut pieces back in and put the delightful butter to one side. Do not taste it! Or, yeah, okay then. A little bit.

2. Now it's time to make the grape jelly. Put the grapes and water in a saucepan and simmer over a medium heat until the fruit starts to get juicy. Simmer for another 10 minutes at the same time as you smash them to smithereens with a masher. Pour out the whole shebang into a steam juicer – or tip into a muslin covered sieve over a large bowl – and leave to drip down into the bowl until you've got at least 600ml/1 pint/generous 2½ cups pure grape juice.

3. Pour this into a saucepan. Squeeze in the lemon, add the sugar and bring to the boil. Let it boil vigorously for a while so that the pectin in the jam sugar can do its job and make the juice deliciously jelly. It should really boil it until it reaches 105°C/220°F, but if you can't face checking the temperature on a thermometer, you can pour a couple of drops onto something ice cold in the fridge and check to see if it sets. When it seems to be ready, you pour it into a jar and put it in the fridge overnight to allow the jelly to set.

4. When it's time to eat, butter the bread, spread on peanut butter and jelly, whack the bread slices together and eat with a large glass of ice-cold milk. XOXO, Jonas.

Bourbon French toast

Poor knights, pain perdu, arme ritter, eggy bread or torrijas — the tradition of dipping old, dry bread in egg and milk and, as if by a flick of a wand, transform it into a combination of breakfast and dessert is found in loads of cultures. For this version, I use bourbon, orange, vanilla and cinnamon — a flavour combination that everyone knows goes as well together as, no, better together than, love and kisses.

Makes 4 slices

4 slices of Pain de Mie
 (see page 12)
4 eggs
150ml/5fl oz/
 scant ⅔ cup milk
3 tbsp freshly squeezed
 orange juice
1 tbsp granulated sugar
1 tbsp cinnamon
2 tbsp bourbon
1 vanilla pod
oil and butter for frying
icing sugar
maple syrup

1. Whisk together the egg, milk, orange juice, sugar, cinnamon and bourbon until well combined — no streaks of egg white should be visible. Cut the vanilla pod in half, scrape out the vanilla seeds and add to the mixture. Pour everything in a square, dip-friendly dish. Add the bread slices and leave them to soak up the mixture for at least 2–3 minutes. You see, a perfect French toast is creamy in the centre and then firmer the closer you get to the crispy surface, so don't just do a quick dip and turn.

2. Add a little oil and lots of butter to a medium-hot frying pan. Take out the bread from the batter and fry gently for 3–4 minutes on each side. If your pan is too hot you'll burn the toast, and if too cold it will dry out — so keep an eye out.

3. Put the slices on a serving plate. Spoon some icing sugar into a sieve and create a beautiful snowfall over them. Serve with maple syrup and a large cup of coffee.

CARAMELISED BANANA

If you want, you can do like they do in New Orleans and eat your French toast with these wonderfully decadent bananas instead of the maple syrup. It goes, of course, just as well together with a pile of newly fried American pancakes.

SERVES 2

3 ripe bananas
2 tbsp butter
2 tbsp dark soft brown sugar
100ml/3½fl oz/scant ½ cup
orange juice
2 tbsp bourbon (optional)

Slice the bananas and fry in the butter in a frying pan over a medium heat. Add the sugar, juice and bourbon, lower the heat and leave to simmer for about 10 minutes until sticky and caramelised.

FROM SCRATCH: KETCHUP

*Makes 1 litre/1¾ pints/
4⅓ cups*

500g/2lb 4oz apples
3 × 400g/14oz cans of
  whole tomatoes
3 brown onions
350g/12oz/1½ cups
  demerara sugar
200ml/7fl oz/scant 1 cup
  apple cider vinegar
1 tbsp salt
1 tsp cayenne pepper
6 black peppercorns
6 whole allspice
6 whole cloves

ST JOHNS KETCHUP Ketchup derives from the
Cantonese word for 'brine from pickled fish'. Western
merchants in the eighteenth century brought the
Chinese habit with them to have a bottle of sweet-
sour-salty fish sauce as a condiment on the table for
livening up boring dishes, and through the years,
the sauce has developed to the tomato sugar bomb
we today call ketchup. There are indeed occasions
when commercial ketchup works perfectly, but in
a sandwich context it's almost always tastier with
home-made. This is a variation of the one that Fergus
Henderson serves in his London restaurant, St John.

1. Peel, deseed and chop the apples. Add all the ingredients to a
   saucepan and leave to simmer gently for about 2 hours, or until
   everything has softened.
2. Leave to cool, take out the spices and blend until smooth.
   Pour back into the saucepan and simmer to reduce to a sticky,
   ketchup consistency.

1–2 dried ancho chillies
200g tube of tomato
  purée
350ml/12fl oz/
  scant 1½ cups water
2 tsp smoked paprika
1 tsp garlic powder
100ml/3½fl oz/
  scant ½ cup white
  wine vinegar
115g/4oz/½ cup
  granulated sugar
1 tsp Worcestershire
  sauce
salt and freshly ground
  black pepper

CUBAN KETCHUP A simpler version of ketchup
you'll find in, for example, Cuban pressed
sandwiches and in the famous frita. It gets a
nice kick from the chilli and a deep, smoky
flavour from the Spanish paprika. Very tasty.

1. Remove the stalks and seeds from the chilli. Put the chilli and
   the rest of the ingredients into a saucepan and simmer
   together into a sticky ketchup consistency.
2. Leave to cool, then blend until smooth. Season
   to taste with salt and pepper.

FROM SCRATCH: MUSTARD

75g/3oz/½ cup yellow
  mustard seeds
100ml/3½fl oz/
  scant ½ cup white
  wine vinegar
100ml/3½fl oz/
  scant ½ cup white wine
1 tbsp maple syrup
1 tsp turmeric
1 tsp salt
1 tsp cayenne pepper

JOE BEEF MUSTARD To make home-made mustard is incredibly easy. You just have to leave mustard seeds to soak in some kind of liquid (water, wine or why not home-brewed IPA) for a couple of days and then blend. And since the basic principle is so simple, it's also easy to experiment. And it's tasty! Here, for example, is a very yummy variety from the Joe Beef pub in Quebec.

1. Mix all the ingredients together in a stainless steel bowl and leave to stand for 2 days.
2. Blend to the required coarseness. If the mustard is too thick, thin it out with some water.

75g/3oz/½ cup brown
  mustard seeds
75g/3oz/½ cup yellow
  mustard seeds
500ml/17fl oz/generous
  2 cups water
200ml/7fl oz/scant 1 cup
  apple cider vinegar
100g/3½oz/heaped ¾
  cup mustard powder
2 tbsp brown sugar
1 tbsp salt
½ tsp ground cinnamon
½ tsp ground allspice
½ tsp ground ginger
1 tsp turmeric
2 garlic cloves

DELI MUSTARD If you want a wholegrain, slightly spicier mustard of the same kind that you get on your sandwich at a New York deli, you just have to follow this recipe. It keeps fresh for a couple of weeks in the fridge.

1. Mix together mustards seeds and water in a stainless steel bowl. Cover and leave to soak in the fridge for a couple of days.
2. Add the rest of the ingredients and pour into a saucepan. Simmer gently, without a lid, until the liquid has reduced by a quarter. Blend quickly, for 30 seconds maximum – the mustard should still be quite coarse.

31

FROM SCRATCH: MAYONNAISE

2 eggs
2 tsp white wine vinegar
2 tsp Dijon mustard
500ml/17fl oz/generous
    2 cups rapeseed oil
salt

MAYONNAISE The world is made up of two kinds of people: those who love mayo, and those who haven't yet understood the simple geniality of the most widespread emulsion in the world. When it comes to mayo, I have this advice to give: buy American, buy Japanese, or make it yourself. And if you make it yourself, make sure all your ingredients are at room temperature. Here is a simple basic recipe.

1. Whisk together the eggs, vinegar and mustard. While mixing constantly, add the oil in a thin, thin stream. This may sound a lot for 2 eggs, but all of it should go in. You see, this will make the mayo thicker, whiter and yummier – and if it gets too thick it's easy to just stir in a little water.
2. Season with salt. This will keep for a couple of weeks in the fridge.

Makes 500ml/17fl oz/ generous 2 cups

2 garlic cloves
3 spring onions
300ml/10½fl oz/generous
    1¼ cups Mayonnaise
    (see page 32)
2 tbsp Dijon mustard
2 tbsp wholegrain Dijon
    mustard
1 tbsp finely chopped
    parsley
1 tbsp Tabasco sauce
2 tsp finely chopped capers
1 tsp Worcestershire sauce
1 tsp paprika
3 tbsp finely chopped
    gherkins
3 tbsp finely chopped
    pickled pearl onions

40 THOUSAND BILLION ISLAND SAUCE This turbo-fuelled combination of standard thousand island, deli sauce, Russian dressing, and New Orleans' spicy hot tartar sauce is my secret sandwich weapon. It goes with almost anything. If you also choose to make it with Kewpie mayo, the sauce gets so addictive it runs a risk of being classed as a narcotic. Now I exaggerate – sorry!

1. Finely chop the garlic and spring onions.
2. Mix together all the ingredients to a chunky sauce. Spread onto your sandwich.

Marble
RYE

No, this is not a marble chocolate sponge but a classic Jewish caraway-scented rye bread — the kind you get if you order a sandwich from a deli in New York's East Village. In fact, the marble rye bread has been made immortal in an episode of the TV series *Seinfeld*, where Jerry robs an old lady just to get hold of one — and that's exactly how delicious it is. Old-lady-robbingly good.

Marble rye

Marble rye bread gets its characteristic look from mixing cocoa powder into half the dough, which you then swirl together with the light dough before baking. It's possible, of course, to make the whole bread either light or dark but ... why? When this is so stunning? I normally bake this bread in a big loaf tin, but if you haven't got one of those you can shape it into a loaf by hand.

Makes a 900g/2lb loaf

FOR LIGHT BREAD

75 g/3oz/½ cup rye flour
560g/1lb 4oz/4½ cups
    strong white bread flour
1½ tsp salt
2 tsp fast-action dried yeast
1½ tsp caraway seeds
300ml/10½fl oz/generous
    1¼ cups water
1 tbsp golden syrup
2 tbsp olive oil, plus extra
    to grease

FOR DARK BREAD

75 g/3oz/½ cup rye flour
560g/1lb 4oz/4½ cups
    strong white bread flour
1½ tsp salt
2 tsp dried yeast
1½ tsp caraway seeds
300ml/10½fl oz/generous
    1¼ cups water
1 tbsp black treacle
2 tbsp olive oil
2 tbsp cocoa powder
brown or black food
    colouring (optional)
melted butter, to glaze

1. Start by making the light bread. Mix together the dry ingredients in a dough mixer bowl. Add water, syrup and oil and knead for about 8 minutes, twice that long if you are doing it by hand. Shape the dough into a large bun, place it in an oiled bowl and cover with clingfilm.

2. Repeat for the dark bread, but stir the cocoa powder into the dry ingredients, and a few drops of brown or black food colouring, if you want an even darker colour, into the wet ingredients before mixing them. Leave both doughs to rise until doubled in size, about 2 hours.

3. Halve each of the doughs so that you get four doughs in total. Shape them into buns, cover with a tea towel and leave to rest for 20 minutes. Roll them out into about the same-sized ovals, about 1cm/½in thick, and layer them on top of each other, alternating between dark and light. Roll the dough lengthways to a brown-white cylinder shape, making sure you squeeze out any air in between the layers. Shape into a loaf by hand or place the dough in a greased tin that is slightly larger than a standard loaf tin and leave to rise until doubled in size, about 90 minutes.

4. Preheat the oven to 180°C/350°F/gas 4. Make 3 diagonal cuts on the loaf using a super-sharp knife and bake in the centre of the oven for about 45 minutes. Leave to cool completely, then brush with a little melted butter.

VARIATION

If you use the brown dough outwards, the loaf will be brown and vice versa. You can also make a completely brown or completely light loaf – depending on what you feel like.

THE SANDWICH LOVER'S GUIDE TO KITCHEN UTENSILS

Bread knife. Even knife nerds tend to neglect their bread knives, but to invest in a really good one will actually give you prettier bread slices and increased cutting satisfaction.

Broad spatula. This super-heavy spatula is good if you want completely flat bacon, and for making burgers or pressed sandwiches. Can be replaced by a grill press or a brick wrapped in kitchen foil (really!).

Ham knife. The dream is, of course, to have your own ham-cutting machine, but if you want properly thinly cut meat without spending too much money, a ham knife is a good alternative. Works like a less flexible fillet knife.

Frying pan with lid. You won't need an expensive and ugly sandwich grill to make really good sandwiches at home; a good frying pan equipped with a lid – that you use when you want your cheese to melt, for example – is enough.

Reuben sandwich

Just like the original sandwich, the Reuben sandwich was invented to be eaten during poker games – although this one wasn't constructed by a British lord but by a Lithuanian immigrant. Today it's perhaps the most iconic of deli sandwiches and comes in an abundance of more or less unholy versions. This is how to make a damned fine version, in my opinion.

Makes 4 sandwiches

8 slices of Marble Rye (see page 36)
sauerkraut, to taste
butter for frying
16 slices of Appenzeller cheese
40 Thousand Billion Island Dressing (see page 32)

FOR THE SALT BEEF

1.5–2kg/3lb 5oz–4lb 8oz cured brisket (see page 52)
1 tsp whole allspice
1 tsp mustard seeds
1 tsp coriander seeds
1 tsp chilli flakes
1 tsp black peppercorns
½ tsp cardamom seeds
2 dried bay leaves
1 tsp ground ginger
2cm/¾in cinnamon stick

1. Start by making salt beef by placing a chunk of cured brisket into a pan and adding water until the meat is covered by about 5cm/1¾in – this is to make sure it doesn't get too salty. Add the spices to the water and leave to simmer gently for 3–4 hours or until the meat is tender and nice. Take out the meat and leave to cool. Will keep fresh in the fridge for up to a week. Strain and reserve the stock – it's perfect for freezing to use when you fancy a quick noodle broth.

2. When Reuben-time is approaching, preheat the oven to 180°C/350°F/gas 4 and slice the cold meat against the grain as thinly as you possibly can. Fry the sauerkraut in a knob of butter. Put a couple of slices of cheese on each slice of bread, then put them in the oven for a few minutes and leave the cheese to melt – you'll want the cheese to melt and the bread to be warm but still soft.

3. Assemble the sandwiches by spooning on a dollop of 40 thousand billion island dressing, fried sauerkraut and finally a generous amount of finely sliced salt beef – think like a New York deli rather than a stingy Swedish café. Finish off with another slice of bread, cut into triangles and eat. What (possibly) is left over of the meat, you'll of course save for other sandwiches or just for nibbling on when raiding the fridge.

4. If you'd like you can just as well eat your Reuben grilled. Then it'll go amazingly crispy and cheese melty instead of soft and smooth. For this, fry the assembled sandwich over medium heat and with a weight on top – 5–6 minutes each side will usually do it.

OTHER FAMOUS REUBENS

WEST COAST REUBEN
Swap the 40 thousand billion island dressing for Dijon mustard.

MONTREAL REUBEN
Swap salt beef for Pastrami (see page 40).

GEORGIA REUBEN
Swap salt beef for Pastrami, the 40 thousand billion island dressing for barbecue sauce and the sauerkraut for coleslaw. And there's also Rachel See page 42.

Pastrami on rye

A pastrami on rye made according all known rules just has to be the world's tastiest sandwich — without any competition. But just like a perfect hamburger or a grilled cheese sandwich, it's such a simple construction that the smallest amount of cheating is immediately noticed. So, here you must make everything from scratch I'm afraid. Plus, you will need a smoker.

Makes 4 sandwiches

8 slices of Marble Rye (see page 36)
about 2kg/4lb 8oz cured brisket (see page 52)
1 tbsp coriander seeds
1 tbsp black peppercorns
hickory or apple wood smoking chips (or a combination)
mustard (see page 31)

1. To make sure it is not too salty, soak the salt beef in water for 1½ hours. Drain off the water and pat the meat dry. Toast the coriander seeds and black pepper in a hot, dry frying pan until it smells lovely, then crush the spices into a fine powder using a pestle and mortar or a spice mill. Pat the meat with the ground spice mixture. There should be plenty of it.

2. Set up your grill or smoker for indirect grilling. Heat it up to 110–120°C/230–250°F and make sure the temperature is consistent. Throw in a handful of wood smoking chips, place the meat on the rack and close the lid. Pastrami can take a lot of smoke, so throw in more chips when the first lot has stopped smoking. Barbecue until the inside temperature has reached about 65°C.150°F, about 3 hours. Take out and leave to cool.

3. Before serving, heat the oven to 140°C and place a deep dish filled with water in the oven. Place the meat on a rack just above and steam it until it becomes super-tender, about 2–4 hours.

4. Take out, slice thinly and place an embarrassing amount of the heavenly meat between two slices untoasted rye with just a little mustard on top. Make sure you include all three parts of the pastrami in each sandwich: the delightful tender and bright red meat, the crispy smoky edges and the lovely fat. I'm drooling ...

»I find pastrami to be the most sensual of all the salted cured meats.«

– George Costanza's girlfriend Vivian, Seinfeld

Rachel sandwich

A Rachel sandwich is essentially a Reuben but with coleslaw instead of sauerkraut and pastrami instead of salt beef. If you've smoked a lot of pastrami anyway you'll have to try making one of these. Super-tasty! I normally make my Rachel sandwiches using completely brown rye, as it looks so nice together with the bright red coleslaw. But you can, of course, do what you want. As you've always done.

Makes 4 sandwiches

8 slices of Marble Rye (see page 36)
40 Thousand Billion Island Sauce (see page 32)
Pastrami (see page 40)
Deli Coleslaw (see page 55)
Dill Pickles (see page 113)

1. Spread some sauce on 4 slices of bread, cover with an American large amount of freshly steamed pastrami and top with coleslaw, some more sauce and another slice of bread. Cut in half, not diagonally, and serve together with dill pickles.

2. If you want you can, of course, just as well eat your Rachel hot. If so, fry the assembled sandwich with a weight on top on medium heat – 5–6 minutes per side is normally fine.

SEITAN – VEGAN PASTRAMI

480g/1lb 1oz/4¾ cups wheat gluten flour
2 tbsp nutritional yeast
60g/2¼oz/½ cup plain flour
1 tsp salt
1 tsp ground cumin
1 tbsp paprika
3 brown onions, sliced
2 tbsp olive oil
3 tbsp Chinese soy sauce
2 tbsp Chilli Sauce (see page 124)
1 litre/1¾ pints/4⅓ cups water
2 tsp finely chopped fresh coriander
2 tsp freshly ground black pepper
hickory smoking chips

Surprise the vegetarian in your life with this smoky vegan pastrami. You can find wheat gluten flour and nutritional yeast in health food shops.

1. Start by mixing the dry ingredients together in the dough mixer bowl. Fry the onions in the oil in a frying pan until soft. Add 2 tbsp of the soy sauce, the chilli sauce and half the water, then blend until smooth. Pour this into the flour mixture and run the dough mixer until you get a springy dough – up to 30 minutes.

2. Preheat the oven to 180°C/350°F/gas 4. Form the dough into a loaf shape; the ambitious form into a brisket shape (or Texas shape?). Squeeze out any surplus water and place the dough in an oven dish. Add the remaining soy sauce to the remaining water, then pour it over the dough, whack it in the oven and bake for 60 minutes. Take the seitan out of the dish and leave to cool. Wrap in clingfilm and leave in the fridge overnight.

3. The next day, prepare your grill for indirect grilling. 110–120°C/230–250°F is usually fine. Pat the seitan with equal amounts of coriander and black pepper. Throw a couple of handfuls of hickory wood smoking chips on the grill and barbecue for 1½ hours. Once done, you slice it thinly and use instead of pastrami in lots of delicious sandwiches. It keeps fresh for a week in the fridge.

Chopped liver sandwich

'What am I? Chopped liver?' George Costanza's dad in *Seinfeld*, just like so many other New Yorkers, used to say this when he felt a bit overlooked in social situations. Perhaps the saying comes from the fact that this deli sandwich always has been standing in the shade of the other, more boastful, sandwiches in this chapter. But a well-executed chopped liver can be just as nice, I promise.

Makes 4 sandwiches

8 slices of Marble Rye (see page 36)
3 brown onions, sliced
Schmaltz and Gribenes (see page 51)
500g/1lb 2oz chicken liver
1 bay leaf
1 fresh thyme sprig
½ tsp ground ginger
½ tsp white pepper
2 eggs
3 spring onions, sliced
2 Pickled Eggs, sliced (see page 112)
Pickled Red Onion (see page 112)
salt

1. Fry the onions until soft in some schmaltz. Add the liver, fry for a little longer and then lower the heat and add the bay leaf, thyme, ginger and pepper. Leave to simmer gently for about 10 minutes. Season to taste with salt. Oh, and use the time to hard boil and shell the eggs too.

2. Take out the bay leaf and thyme sprig from the liver mixture and pour it out onto a chopping board. In the US, you normally get your chopped liver blended, like a home-made liver pâté, but I actually prefer to take the name literally and coarsely chop the liver with a knife together with the onions and the hard-boiled eggs. If you want to be a bit more traditional and blend it, I suggest just to pulse it quickly so that you don't turn the whole thing into cat food.

3. Fry the marble rye in some schmaltz to make it crispy. Top 4 slices with a generous amount of chopped liver, then sliced spring onion, sliced pickled eggs, pickled red onion and a handful of crispy gribenes.

VEGETARIAN
CHOPPED LIVER

During some of the Jewish lent periods, it's tradition not to eat meat and instead prepare this vegetarian variety. If, for some reason, you would like to do the same you just exclude the gribenes and schmaltz and replace the chicken liver with 400g/14oz can of chickpeas, drained, and 75g/3oz/½ cup walnuts that you blend until smooth. For everything else you just do the same, okay?

Chicken salad sandwich

The worst thing I know when it comes to sandwiches is all these revolting mayonnaise-soaked stuffings. Just the words 'mayo filling' make my stomach turn. Mayonnaise is used as a sauce or not at all. Okay? There is, however, one exception: this divine chicken salad sandwich. The trick is to use a minimal amount of mayo and to add lots of fresh crispy stuff to the salad.

Makes 4 sandwiches

8 slices Marble Rye
   (see page 36)
1 whole chicken, about
   1.3kg/3lb
4 spring onions, chopped
3 celery sticks, chopped
100ml/3½fl oz/scant
   ½ cup Mayonnaise
   (see page 32)
a squeeze of lemon
Schmaltz and Gribenes
   (see page 51)
salt and freshly ground
   black pepper

FOR THE QUICK
PICKLED CUCUMBER

1 tbsp distilled vinegar,
   12%
100ml/3½fl oz/scant
   ½ cup water
2 tbsp granulated sugar
1 tsp salt
½ cucumber

1. Butcher the chicken into 4 pieces, 2 breasts and 2 thighs/legs. The wings you can use for something else. Remove the skin and use it for sewing a woman's suit. Just kidding. No, make them into gribenes and schmaltz, of course. Bring salted water to the boil in a big saucepan, add the chicken, cover with a lid and leave to simmer for 40 minutes. Take out and leave to cool.

2. When the chicken is cold, pick the meat off the bones and chop roughly. Place the meat in a bowl and add chopped spring onion and celery. Stir in enough mayo just to coat the other ingredients in a thin layer. Add salt, pepper and lemon juice to taste.

3. To make the cucumber, mix together the distilled vinegar, water, sugar and salt and stir until the sugar has dissolved. Slice the cucumber thinly using either a mandolin or a cheese slicer and add to the pickling brine.

4. Brown a couple of slices of marble rye in a frying pan with a little bit of schmaltz, top the bread with chicken salad and finish off with the quick pickled cucumber and lots of gribenes.

MAKE YOUR OWN
CELERY SODA

The classic drink to go with a genuine Jewish deli sandwich is Dr Brown's Cel-Ray which is – wait for it – celery soda pop! Quite nice actually. If you don't want to go to New York to test it out you can always make your own. Here's how.

200ml/7fl oz/scant 1 cup water
450g/1lb/2 cups granulated sugar
2 tbsp celery seeds
sparkling water

Bring the water to the boil, add sugar and stir until dissolved. Add the celery seeds and leave them to infuse for 1 hour before draining them off. Keep the syrup in the fridge until it's time to drink, when you mix 2 tbsp syrup with 250ml/8fl oz/1 cup sparkling water. Mmmm ... celery soda.

Patty melt

A patty melt takes the hamburger and the caramelised onion from a slider, the melted cheese from a grilled cheese and the rye bread from a Reuben to create the sandwiches' answer to the supergroup Travelling Wilburys (where the onion is Bob Dylan, of course, and the cheese Jeff Lynne). You don't have to make as many sandwiches as on the picture, but it's recommended.

Makes 4 sandwiches

8 slices Marble Rye (see page 36)
400g/14 oz beef mince made from chuck steak
3 brown onions, sliced
butter for frying
1 whole star anis
150g/5oz Comté, Gruyère or Appenzeller cheese, grated
Ketchup (see page 28)
salt and freshly ground black pepper

1. Divide the mince into four and form into patties a bit bigger than the bread slices – do not press. Fry them in a seriously hot cast-iron frying pan without any fat so you get a good caramelisation on the meat, then stand aside and sprinkle with salt and pepper. It doesn't matter if they're still a bit rare.

2. Lower the heat and fry off the onions in butter in the same pan so that you don't waste all the good meat flavour. Add a whole star anis. If you think it takes a long time to get the onion beautifully caramelised, you can add a few tablespoons of water and let it slowly evaporate – it will probably take a total of 30 minutes. Season to taste with salt and pepper.

3. Brown one side of the bread slices in a dry non-stick pan over a medium heat. Add grated cheese to the toasted side, a meat patty, the caramelised onion (remove the star anis), more cheese, and finish off with another slice of bread, with the toasted side facing the cheese. Leaving the sandwich to it, brown off while pressed down under a broad spatula so that the cheese gets time to melt properly – 8 minutes per side is perfect, so make sure your cooker is on a medium heat. Halve the sandwiches and dip in home-made ketchup.

HOW TO MAKE A SMASH BURGER

If you want to make sure you don't get a compact burger, you can use the so-called smash technique to get thin burgers with uneven edges and a good frying surface.

1. Shape freshly ground mince from chuck steak or similar, preferably with 20% fat content, to round balls by hand or with an ice cream scoop. Don't press.

2. Heat up a cast-iron frying pan without adding cooking fat. Add the ball and quickly press down with a broad spatula or similar.

3. Turn over once you've got a nice fried crust. Salt and pepper on the cooked side. You can melt any cheese by covering the frying pan with a lid.

FROM SCRATCH: SCHMALTZ AND GRIBENES

chicken skin
salt

SCHMALTZ AND GRIBENES If you want to make deli sandwiches at home, you'll have to know how to make schmaltz and gribenes, two staples in the Jewish kitchen. Gribenes is crispy chicken skin and is used as a kind of stand-in for bacon, while schmaltz essentially is set chicken fat, which might not sound that super-nice but which is completely heavenly instead of butter on sandwiches or in food. The good news is that it's incredibly cheap and easy to make them both. Yes, you even make them at them same time. Use the skin from chicken you cook, or you may find it very cheaply in food markets or at the butcher's.

1. Spread out the chicken skin on an oven tray and place in the freezer for about 1 hour. This is to make it easier to cut. Take it out and cut the pieces into about 1cm/½in wide strips, then in turn cut the strips into about 1cm/½in squares. Place them on an oven tray and sprinkle over a little salt.

2. Preheat the oven to 180°C/350°F/gas 4. Once hot enough, roast the chicken skin in the centre of the oven for about 20 minutes, but keep an eye on it all the time so that it doesn't burn or it will taste awful. Once all the skin pieces have turned a nice colour and look crispy, take out the baking tray, scoop up the chicken skin, which has now become gribenes, with a slotted spoon and leave to drain on a piece of kitchen paper. Season to taste with salt. The gribenes should be eaten as soon as possible.

2. Strain the chicken fat through a sieve into a bowl and place in the fridge. Season to taste with salt. Once the fat has set, you have schmaltz. Yiha! Schmaltz fest! I will keep nicely in the fridge for up to 2 weeks.

FROM SCRATCH: CURED BRISKET

2 celery sticks, roughly
  chopped
½ carrot, roughly chopped
½ brown onion, roughly
  chopped
5 litres/8¾ pints/20 cups
  water
400g/14oz/2 cups salt
50g curing salt with 0.6%
  sodium nitrite (or 50g
  salt + ½ tbsp saltpetre/
  potassium nitrate)
200g/7oz/¾ cup
  granulated sugar
4 garlic cloves
2 tsp coriander seeds
10 whole allspice
4 whole cloves
1 cinnamon stick
3 bay leaves
2kg/4lb 8oz whole brisket

CURED BRISKET Both smoked pastrami and boiled salt beef is made from the same sort of basic meat: cured brisket. Ready-cured brisket can be bought at most good butcher's and works absolutely fine for when you want to make a good weekday Reuben. However, cured brisket is normally only sold in smaller pieces, so if you want to make pastrami from a whole brisket, you'll probably have to cure it yourself. The same if you want this genuine traditional New York deli curing.

1. Place all the ingredients except the brisket in a large saucepan, bring to the boil, then simmer until the sugar and salt have dissolved. Leave to cool, then chill in the fridge.
2. Place the brisket in a bowl and pour the brine over it. Cover with clingfilm. Leave to cure in the fridge for 5 days. Then follow the instructions for making either pastrami or salt beef.

CURING SALT

Sodium nitrite is used in charcuteries mainly to prevent the food poisoning illness botulism. However, it is very unusual for whole pieces of meat to be contaminated with the bacteria; it's mostly pickled herring, cold smoked fish and, to some extent, ground charcuteries that are in the risk zone. Indeed, the word botulism even comes from the Latin word for sausage. Since there are a few negative health aspects associated with eating too much sodium nitrite, you can exclude this from the recipe if you want – as long as you're being careful with the hygiene. Your salt beef won't turn that beautiful red colour, and your pork belly won't get that same characteristic bacon flavour. Don't forget that sodium nitrite actually appears naturally in certain foods. For example, it's the sodium nitrite in cabbage that makes the mince turn red when making cabbage rolls. In many countries, you can't buy pure sodium nitrite. But saltpetre, which is converted to sodium nitrite in the meat, can be bought in food shops. It can be tricky to control how much sodium nitrite ends up in the meat, so curing salt, containing 0.6% sodium nitrite and the rest cooking salt, can be bought from the butcher or online. Just remember that you can only use it to a maximum of 2.5% of the weight of the meat when making sausages, or 5% when you are dry curing.

HOW TO SPEED UP THE FERMENTING PROCESS

If you're in a hurry and want to eat your home-made sauerkraut after 5 days, there is a shortcut. You see, sauerkraut works a little bit like sourdough: add a little bacteria culture and the fermentation process kicks in a little earlier. You can do this in two ways: you either save some salt brine from an old batch or you buy ready-made sauerkraut and pour a little bit of sauerkraut juice over the home-made batch. Just remember that if you do so, use the kind of sauerkraut that you get from the refrigerated display — those in a jar haven't got the same quality of bacteria.

FROM SCRATCH: COLESLAW AND SAUERKRAUT

½ head red cabbage,
   about 600g/1lb 5oz
1 white onion
¼ celeriac, about
   200 g/7oz
2 carrots

FOR THE BRINE

100ml/3½fl oz/½ cup
   distilled vinegar, 12%
1 tbsp apple cider vinegar
½ tsp fennel seeds
½ tbsp cumin seeds
2 tbsp dark soft brown
sugar
1 tsp salt

DELI COLESLAW In the world of coleslaw there are two factions: those who prefer mixing their cabbage salad with mayonnaise and those who prefer vinegar. I've always been a bit of a mayo guy, but after trying this beautifully red classic deli coleslaw, I've definitely converted. The coleslaw must rest for at least 24 hours, so make sure you're planning ahead. The preparations are, on the other hand, easy.

1. Just slice the red cabbage super-thinly, finely chop the onion and finely shred the celeriac and carrot. Mix everything together in a large bowl.
2. Bring all the ingredients for the brine to the boil. Remove from the heat, leave to steep for 15 minutes, then pour the liquid over the cabbage through a sieve and mix well.
3. Place a plate with a weight on top over the cabbage and leave in the fridge overnight. It keeps fresh for a week.

---

2 litres/3½ pints/
   8¼ cups water
100g/3½oz/½ cup salt
½ head white cabbage,
   about 600g/1lb 5oz

TO SERVE

chicken stock
bay leaf (optional)
caraway seeds (optional)

SAUERKRAUT Sauerkraut is also one of those home-made things that are so much tastier than shop bought.

1. Bring the water and salt to the boil and simmer until the salt has dissolved. Leave to cool.
2. Pour the salt brine over the finely shredded cabbage and mix. Cover with a clean tea towel, place a plate on top and finally a weight that presses down the cabbage in the liquid. Leave the sauerkraut to ferment for 2 weeks, stored in a dark place at room temperature (that is if your home isn't warmer than 23°C/73°F, or bad bacteria can start to grow).
3. After about two weeks, you can test it. The cabbage should be pale and nicely sour-salty but still have a good crunch. Drain off, but keep, the liquid. This should be brought to the boil, cooled down, then poured over the sauerkraut so that it's just covered. Throw the rest away. Keep the sauerkraut in the fridge for up to three weeks.
4. When it's time to eat the sauerkraut, you braise it in equal quantities of salt brine from the jar and stock or water. If you want, you can also add a bay leaf and a few caraway seeds. Bring to the boil, lower the heat and leave to simmer gently for 30 minutes. Serve.

Scones
AND MUFFINS

It's easy to get confused here — I wouldn't want to be in a three-way conversation with an American and an Englishman, that's for sure. A British biscuit is an American cookie, apart from the British biscuits that are called cookies. An American biscuit is a British scone. In the UK, a muffin is most often used for those mega-cupcake-style cakes, while an English muffin, we all understand, is a roll. Okay? Scones — for which you may read biscuits — are tender and break up easily. Perfect, in fact, to make into sandwiches. English muffins are a tougher kind of bread with polenta, which tastes absolutely at its best if toasted first. Both breads are quite interchangeable in the following sandwich recipes, so use whichever variety you fancy.

Biscuits.

Muffins. ————

Scones and muffins

SCONES If you want beautiful, high scones that really melt in your mouth, the trick is to work the dough as little as possible. These are similar to the 'biscuits' popular in the southern US.

Makes 4

300g/11oz/2½ cups strong white bread flour,
    plus extra for dusting
a pinch of bicarbonate of soda
1 tbsp baking powder
1 tsp salt
100g/3½oz cold butter, diced
250ml/9fl oz/generous 1 cup buttermilk

1. Preheat the oven to 220°C/425°F/gas 7. Mix the dry ingredients in a bowl, add the butter and rub it into the flour until it looks like a crumble. You'll get the best results when using a food processor, as there's a smaller chance the butter will melt – just pulse a few times so that the butter is just about mixed in with the flour. Add the buttermilk and stir quickly. Scones get better the more careless you are, so let it be a bit rough.
2. Turn out the very sticky dough onto a floured worktop and carefully press it out with floured hands. Do not roll out. Fold the dough on the centre, press out with your fingers and repeat this about 4 times. Press out the dough one last time until about 4cm/1½in thick. Use something round to cut out four beautiful scones – resist the temptation to throw the rest together to form a last bun. It will never turn out nice.
3. Bake in the centre of the oven for 10–12 minutes, or until the biscuits are beautifully golden brown. Serve immediately.

ENGLISH MUFFINS Called English muffins to distinguish them from the more cakey, mega-cupcake-style cakes, they are possibly more popular in the US than in the UK.

Makes 10 muffins

2 tsp fast-action dried yeast
1 tsp granulated sugar
300ml/10½fl oz/generous 1¼ cups tepid whole milk
55g/2oz butter, melted
450g/1lb/heaped 3½ cups strong white bread flour,
    plus extra for dusting
1 tsp salt
polenta for rolling out
butter for frying

1. Mix together the yeast, sugar, milk and melted butter directly in the dough mixer. Add the flour and salt and mix together to a smooth and springy dough – it'll take about 5 minutes. Transfer to an oiled bowl, cover with a tea towel and leave to rise for 1 hour.
2. Knock the dough back with a buttered, no, a floured, fist. Sprinkle polenta on the work surface, divide the dough into two and roll each part out to about 2cm/¾in thick. Cut out 12 rounds using a 10cm/4in cutter and place on a piece of baking parchment. Leave to rise for another 30 minutes.
3. Heat up a frying pan and add a knob of butter. Fry the muffins over a medium heat for about 5 minutes on each side. Before eating, cut the bread open using a fork and then break into two halves so they get nice and rough. Don't forget to toast them!

Breakfast muffins

The absolutely tastiest fast-food dish is without a doubt an Egg McMuffin. It's common knowledge. But if you neither want to stuff your body full of additives, nor support 'the man' — then what do you do? You make your own breakfast muffins, of course. If you want to make them like they do in the American Southern States, you use a scone. If you want to be a bit more like the city folks, you use an English muffin. Either way you'll get a perfect start to your day.

Serves 4

finest-quality bacon (see page 96)

4 eggs

4 Scones or English muffins (see page 59)

butter for spreading

4 slices of hamburger cheese singles or home-made American cheese (see page 70)

butter

1. Fry the bacon until crispy. If you have round cutter that's about the same size as your scones or muffins, grease it on the inside, place in the frying pan, crack an egg into it and fry until the egg has set so you get a perfect shape. Which can be quite fun, right? If not, just fry like normal.

2. Cut open a freshly baked scone and spread with butter. Place a slice of cheese on the bottom half, followed by bacon, the fried egg and finally, the top half. Eat. Enjoy.

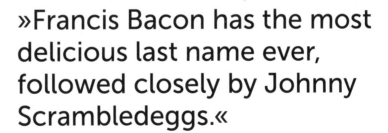

»Francis Bacon has the most delicious last name ever, followed closely by Johnny Scrambledeggs.«

— Jarod Kintz, author

Eggs Benedict

Eggs Benedict is universally super-tasty, a little bit like the sandwiches equivalent to *Breaking Bad*. Eggs Benedict is also the most romantic breakfast dish with which you can surprise your loved one, so do that.

Makes 4 sandwiches

8 slices of finest-quality bacon (see page 96), or other ham
2 Scones or English Muffins (see page 59)
4 fresh eggs
distilled vinegar, 12%, for poaching

FOR THE SIMPLE HOLLANDAISE

3 egg yolks
1 tbsp freshly squeezed lemon juice
½ tsp salt
150g/5oz butter
a few drops of Tabasco sauce

1. Start with the part that really qualifies Eggs Benedict to join the sandwiches' Hall of Fame: the hollandaise sauce. I mean, how many sandwiches come smothered in sauce? This simplified hollandaise version is easy to crack if you've got two things: an electric whisk and a tiny bit of patience. Here's how to do it. Whisk the egg yolks together with lemon juice and salt for about 1 minute. Melt the butter and add a little at a time while constantly whisking until a lovely sauce appears. If it gets too thick, you can thin it out with a little water. Add a dash of Tabasco, to taste.

2. Fry the bacon. You could pretty much use almost any kind of ham, but I like bacon. Simple, classic, crispy. An old housewife's tip is to cook the bacon on a rack in the oven. Partly because the fat will drip off, partly because the bacon will get nice and wavy. Leave to drain on a piece of kitchen paper, then place on top of a halved scone.

3. Some people seem to think it's tricky to poach eggs. It's not. At least not if the egg is really fresh – old eggs don't quite hold together. You just have to crack the egg into a little cup or something. Bring water to the boil in a saucepan, add a dash of vinegar and then stir the water with a wooden spoon until you've made a little whirl. Then quickly drop the egg down into the water, cover the pan with a lid and leave it there for 3 minutes before taking it out with a slotted spoon to put on top of your sandwich. The white will then be creamy and the yolk runny. Mmm. Slowly and sensually, pour the sauce over the sandwich and voilà! Eggs Benedict.

OTHER FAMOUS EGGS BENEDICT

EGGS FLORENTINE
Replace the ham with blanched spinach.

EGGS ROYALE
Replace the ham with smoked salmon.

OSCAR BENEDICT
Replace the ham with boiled asparagus and crabmeat.

HUEVOS BENEDICTOS
Replace the ham with raw Spanish chorizo formed into a patty and fried, and top with both hollandaise and hot salsa.

Fried chicken scones

Fried chicken with honey-mustard sauce is one of those flavour combinations which really marry, and celebrate their wedding night in your mouth. Wonderful! And it will get even better, of course, if served in a proper Southern State scone. Take the opportunity to make a bit extra so that you get to experience the simple pleasure of sneaking out into the kitchen late at night to snack on fridge-cold fried chicken.

Makes 4 sandwiches

4 Scones (see page 59)
4 chicken thighs on
   the bone
250ml/9fl oz/generous
   1 cup buttermilk
1½ tsp salt
2 tsp finely grated
   lemon zest
2 tsp freshly squeezed
   lemon juice
210g/7½oz/scant
   1¾ cups plain flour
1¼ tsp garlic powder
1¼ tsp onion powder
1 tsp freshly ground
   black pepper
1 tsp paprika
1 tsp dried thyme
¼ tsp cayenne pepper
rapeseed oil, for
   deep-frying
55g/2oz butter
2 tbsp clear honey
2 tbsp wholegrain
   Dijon mustard
Pickled Gherkins or Dill
   Pickles (see page 113)

1. Cut the bone off the chicken thighs so that you end up with one whole piece of meat, and pull off the skin and save for schmaltz (see page 51). Mix together the buttermilk, salt, lemon zest and juice in a bowl. Mix together flour and the dry spices in another bowl, or preferably, in a paper bag. Dip the chicken thighs first in the buttermilk mixture and then in the flour mixture. If you have a paper bag, shake the thighs in it until the pieces are completely coated in flour.

2. Fill a cast-iron frying pan to one-third full with oil and heat to about 165°C/330°F. Deep-fry the chicken until golden brown, about 8 minutes. Take out of the pan and leave to drain on a piece of kitchen paper. Sprinkle with salt.

3. Melt the butter, honey and mustard in a saucepan over a medium heat until a magic honey-mustard sauce appears. Cut a freshly baked scone in half, add a fried piece of chicken and about five slices of pickled gherkins on the bottom half. Pour over the honey-mustard sauce, place the other scone half on top and serve immediately.

PIMENTO CHEESE SCONES

Pimento cheese, or 'the caviar of the South', is a kind of home-made cheese dip, which is incredibly popular in the American South. Of course, it's very nice served in a scone with some bacon, chilli and tomato.

MAKES 4 SCONES

4 Scones (see page 59)
8 slices of finest-quality bacon
(see page 96)
Pickled Chilli (see page 113)
4 slices of tomato
For the pimento cheese
375g/13oz/3 cups grated Gouda cheese
200g/7oz cream cheese
100g/3½oz grilled peppers from a jar
3 tbsp Mayonnaise (see page 32)
1 tsp turmeric
1 tsp Chilli Sauce (see page 124)
½ tsp celery salt

Blend the ingredients for the pimento cheese together until you get a cheesy batter. Fry the bacon crispy, then drain off on kitchen paper. Spread pimento onto a freshly baked scone, add jalapeño, tomato and bacon. Eat.

Biscuits with red eye gravy

If you are standing there with a cup of coffee in your hand frying bacon anyway, why not pour a little in and make it into a sauce? Yes, this was probably how this super-simple Southern State favourite was born. The combination of coffee and smoked pork might be a flavour that you'd have to grow up with to appreciate, but it was Elvis' — and an abundance of truck drivers' — favourite brekkie, and that's good enough for me.

Makes 2 sandwiches

2 Scones (see page 59)
4 slices of finest-quality bacon or smoked ham (see page 96)
150ml/5fl oz/scant ⅔ cup hot black coffee
1 tbsp brown sugar
2 tbsp butter
salt

1. Fry the bacon or smoked ham. If you use bacon, fry until crispy. If you end up with too much fat in the pan you can pour some out if you want.
2. Carefully measure the coffee in a cup, and then pretend to just be standing there casually sipping it. Whisk the sugar into the frying pan and then, as nonchalant as you possibly can, pour the cup of coffee down the frying pan. It will look ace. Bring to the boil and reduce until the sauce thickens. Stir in the butter to make it smooth and shiny. Season to taste with a little salt, but remember that the bacon/ham is salty as well.
3. Place the ham or the bacon onto a scone cut in half. Pour over the sauce. Eat immediately.

SCONES AND GRAVY

That is, scones smothered in a kind of thick béchamel sauce. This, of course, sounds crazy but is actually quite nice. This is how to do it.

MAKES 2 SANDWICHES

2 Scones (see page 59)
2 fresh pork sausages
2 tbsp butter
2 tbsp plain flour
200ml/7fl oz/scant 1 cup whole milk
salt and freshly ground black pepper

Remove the skin from the sausages and tear the sausage meat into small pieces. Fry the pieces until crispy in a frying pan over a medium heat. Add the butter, then the flour, stirring all the time, and finally milk. Leave the sauce to thicken, stirring. Season to taste with salt and pepper. Cut a scone in half and pour over the sauce. Eat immediately.

Scotch egg scones

A Scotch egg is a classic British pub snack that's made up of a soft-boiled egg wrapped in sausage meat and then fried. I'm not sure which smartass came up with the idea to put it in a Southern State scone, but I have to say I like their thinking. Bring one of these sandwiches to the picnic and I promise no one will forget it. Ever. Eat with a beer.

Makes 4 sandwiches

4 Scones (see page 59)
6 eggs
2 garlic cloves
2 tbsp grated horseradish
4 fresh pork sausages
100g/3½oz/1 cup panko breadcrumbs
125g/4½oz/1 cup plain flour
vegetable oil for deep-frying
Mustard (see page 31)

1. The secret to a really good Scotch egg is a runny yolk while the white is firm and the sausage meat, of course, is cooked through. A bit tricky. So how do you do it, then? Well, you follow these instructions meticulously and keep your fingers crossed. This is how to do it: place 4 of the eggs in a saucepan filled with water. Bring to the boil and immediately take the pan off the heat and leave to stand for 3 minutes before plunging the eggs in ice-cold water to halt the cooking process and then shelling them.

2. Using a pestle and mortar, crush the garlic with the horseradish into a paste. Remove the skin from the sausages and shape into four balls. Place each ball on a piece of clingfilm and flatten out until about 5mm/¼in thick. Spread the garlic and horseradish paste on top and then place a shelled soft-boiled egg on top, so it stands up in the centre of the meat. Grip the four edges of the clingfilm and fold upwards so that the flattened meat sort of automatically covers the egg. Remove the clingfilm, remove any overlapping meat and cover up any holes. But be careful so the egg doesn't burst.

3. Whisk the remaining two eggs. Pour the panko onto a plate and the flour onto another. Roll the eggs in the flour, then in the egg and finally in the panko. Make sure all the eggs are coated in an even layer of panko.

4. Heat the frying oil to 170°C/340°F. Deep-fry the eggs until golden and crispy, 7–10 minutes in total. Turn over when needed. Leave to drain on a piece of kitchen paper.

5. Cut your scones in half, spread with some good mustard, place a Scotch egg in between and then try to fit it all into your mouth.

FROM SCRATCH: AMERICAN CHEESE

Makes a 200g/7oz cheese

350g/12oz grated Gouda
   or other mild cheese
   with high fat content
1 tbsp powdered milk
½ tsp salt
150ml/5fl oz/scant ⅔ cup
   whole milk
1½ tsp gelatine powder
1 tbsp water

What do you do if you want a soft, creamy cheese with perfect melting qualities without it being plastic-wrapped, tasteless and jam-packed with additives? You make your own American cheese, of course. This recipe, from the wholesome TV programme *America's Test Kitchen*, works incredibly well from ingredients you can find in most food stores. And best of all: as it's made from tasty bought cheese you can choose yourself what you'd like your perfect hamburger or grilled cheese to taste like.

1. Line a 10cm/4in tin with clingfilm. Mix together the Gouda, powdered milk and salt until you get a cheesy mixture. If you want to experiment with a different cheese, remember that it needs to have a high fat content and can't be too matured.
2. Heat up the milk and add the cheese, while stirring until everything has melted. Dissolve the gelatine powder in the water, then add to the cheese mixture. Stir thoroughly. Pour the cheese mixture into the tin, as quick as a flash before it sets again.
3. Place in the fridge overnight. When it's melted cheese time, cut the cheese into thin slices with a sharp knife and prepare to be amazed at how elegantly it melts.

litres/5¼ pints/
13¼ cups organic full
cream milk, raw or
unhomogenised
tsp citric acid
tbsp water
tsp rennet
tsp salt

Creamy home-made mozzarella is very special. This super-easy version is best eaten straight away, but will keep for a day or so in salt brine.

1. Carefully warm the milk to about 12°C/54°F while stirring. Dissolve the citric acid in the water and then pour the mixture into the milk. Continue warming the milk while stirring constantly until it reaches 32°C/90°F, when you add the rennet and stir thoroughly. Soon the milk will start to curdle. Warm to 35–40 degrees and when the curd starts to come off the edges, turn the heat off. Leave to rest for 5 minutes.

2. Slice the curd with a knife all the way to the bottom into 2cm/¾in cubes. Leave to rest for 2–3 minutes. Transfer the curds to a sieve using a slotted spoon and leave the whey to drain off – or save it for using in baking. Sprinkle the salt over the curds.

3. Heat a couple of litres of water to 80°C/176°F. Pour into a bowl or large tin and add the curds. Put on a pair of brand new rubber gloves and squeeze out the last of the whey from the curds and work until a shiny and stretchy mozzarella cheese appears as if by magic. Shape into small round mozzarella balls, or if you can't be bothered, just one big lump. Eat immediately.

1 Baguette (see page 78)
1 beef tomato
olive oil
2 garlic cloves
100ml/3½fl oz/scant ½ cup
Mayonnaise (see page 32)
a bunch of fresh basil
1 ball of Mozzarella, about
115g/4oz (see page 72)
salt and freshly ground
black pepper

CAPRESE

The world's simplest and tastiest sandwich.

Preheat the oven to 150°C/300°F/gas 2. Slice the tomato into about 1cm/½in thick slices. Drizzle over some olive oil, add salt and pepper and roast them with the garlic for about 45 minutes. Squeeze the garlic out of the skins and blend together with the mayo and all but a couple of the basil leaves. Scrape out some of the crumb and toast the baguette quickly in the centre of the oven. Spread with the mayo mixture, add tomato slices and mozzarella. Also add the reserved basil leaves. Add salt and pepper to taste.

Enjoy
Saint

Every, which

– Warren Zevon

Baguettes

To eat a sourdough baguette baked to perfection with just a little butter can be a sublime experience. They're quite useless as sandwich bread, however. They're too tough, too bready, have too big holes in them and the way-too-thick crust gets stuck to the top of your mouth. No, the perfect sandwich baguette has instead a soft crumb and a thin, super-crispy crust.

Banh mi-baguette

To get the perfect sandwich baguette right is more difficult than you might think, but if you follow this recipe exactly you should be able to pull it off. The extra-fine T55 flour – from specialist suppliers or online – means that the bread will get both a light and airy texture, and the steaming will give it a thin but crispy crust. So don't take any shortcuts.

Makes 2 large baguettes

2 tsp fast-action dried yeast
350ml/12fl oz/1½ cups tepid water
540g/1lb 3oz/4½ cups extra-fine wheat flour (T55 flour), plus extra for dusting
1½ tsp salt
1 tbsp granulated sugar

1. Mix together yeast and water straight in the dough mixer bowl. Add the flour, salt and sugar and run for about 2 minutes until the dough is smooth. Knead the dough for double the time if you are doing it by hand. Shape the dough into a ball, put back into the bowl, cover with clingfilm or a lid and leave to rise for about 1 hour until the dough has nearly doubled in size.

2. Flour the back of your hand and knock back the poor dough to squeeze all air out of it. Cover with clingfilm again and leave to rise for another hour. Knock back and leave to rise one more time.

3. Take out the dough and place on a floured worktop. Divide into two. Form the baguettes by pressing them out to a (very rough) rectangle, about 10 x 2cm/4 x 8in, and fold the upper and lower long edges so they meet in the centre. Geddit? If you do, squeeze the seam together and roll the dough into a long thin sausage, about 30cm/12in long.

4. Transfer the baguettes to a baguette tray (or a standard tray) and make sure that the seam is facing downwards. Cover with a tea towel and leave to rise for 30 minutes. Meanwhile, fill a spray bottle with water and preheat the oven to 220°C/425°F/gas 7, and place a deep oven dish filled with water at the bottom of the oven – the steam is there so make sure the right crispy crust appears. So don't skip this step.

5. After 30 minutes make cuts in the baguettes using a very sharp knife or a shaving blade – three diagonal cuts for a po'boy and one long cut for a banh mi. Spray the breads 4–6 times with the water and then bake in the oven for 25 minutes in total. After 3 minutes, open carefully and spray with water, leave to bake for a further 3 minutes, after which you open and spray one more time. After a total of 20 minutes, or until they've started colour nicely, take out the breads and loosen them from the baguette tray. Pop them back in the oven upside-down and bake for 5 minutes so that the bottom gets crispy too.

6. Take out and leave to rest. They're absolutely perfect after 30 minutes. If you wait longer you'll have to warm them up in the oven again to achieve maximum crunch.

THE SANDWICH LOVER'S GUIDE TO THE CHEESE SHOP

1, 3 and 5. Appenzeller, Comté and Gruyère. The sandwich lover's secret trinity. They have perfect melting qualities and a fantastic flavour. Choose a mature one when you want the cheese to stand out, and a milder one when you just want it to linger around kicking a few stones in the background. *2. Mozzarella.* If you don't want a squeaky, compact cheese in your sandwiches there's a lot of superb artisan cheese out there. Buy it! The cheese should preferably be at room temperature when served. *4. British Red Leicester/mild Cheddar.* If you want a more subtle flavour, and better melting qualities, choose a mild, not mature British cheddar. *6. Provolone.* A mild Italian cheese with very good melting qualities and often sold in the shape of a round sausage – ideal for round sandwiches. *7. Parmesan.* Italian hard cheese. Used in sandwiches because of its flavour and often in combination with cheeses that melt more easily.

Bo tai chanh banh mi

If you've never tried raw meat in a sandwich I think it's about time you do so now. Because bo tai chanh is a super-tasty Vietnamese salad made from lime marinated fillet of beef which is perfect for stuffing in between a couple of super-crispy bread halves. Divine on a hot summer's day.

Makes 4 sandwiches

2 Banh Mi Baguettes (see page 78)
800g/1lb 12oz good-quality fillet of beef
handful salted peanuts
groundnut oil or other deep-fry-friendly oil
6 shallots, thinly sliced
a bunch each of fresh coriander, fresh mint, and fresh Thai basil
a handful of prawn crackers, crushed
Maggi celery soy sauce (optional)
Mayonnaise (see page 32)
butter
salt

FOR THE MARINADE

juice of 4 limes
100ml/3½fl oz/scant ½ cup fish sauce
4 tbsp palm sugar (or granulated sugar)
3 garlic cloves, crushed
1 tbsp grated fresh ginger
1–2 bird's eye chillies, thinly sliced

1. Place the beef fillet in the freezer for at least 1 hour. Make the marinade by mixing together the lime juice, fish sauce, sugar, garlic, ginger and chilli, and stir until the sugar has dissolved. Take out the meat and slice, against the grain, as thinly as possible. Pour over three-quarters of the marinade and leave to marinate for 15 minutes.

2. Crush the peanuts coarsely in a pestle and mortar. Heat the oil to 135°C/275°F and deep-fry the onions until they start to colour, 5–10 minutes. Take out the onions, increase the heat to 180°C/350°F and deep-fry the onion for a couple of seconds until super-crispy. Sprinkle with salt and drain on kitchen paper.

3. Assemble the sandwich! Drain the beef a little. Scrape out a bit of the crumb, and crisp the baguettes up for a short while in the oven. Butter the bottom half and pile on a disgustingly large amount of fresh herbs as a base. Add the meat and finish off with some more herbs, some of the saved marinade, crushed peanuts, fried shallots, crushed prawn crackers, Maggi sauce, and perhaps even more chilli and mayo. Put the top half of the bread on top and serve.

PHO

Vietnamese noodle broth is the perfect side dish for banh mi.

Serves 4
For the broth
2kg/4lb 8oz beef bones
4cm/1½in piece of fresh ginger
1 brown onion, halved
1 cinnamon stick
5 star anise
1½ tbsp salt
100ml/3½fl oz/scant ½ cup fish sauce
For the soup topping
1 lime
1 white onion finely shredded
1 bird's eye chilli, finely shredded
2 shallots, thinly sliced
fresh herbs of your choice
boiled rice noodles

Place the bones in a large pan, cover with water, bring to the boil and simmer for 3 minutes. Pour away the water. Rinse the pan and bones, fill with fresh water and bring to the boil. Simmer for 3½ hours. Preheat the oven to 240°C/475°F/gas 9. Dry-roast the ginger and onion until browned, then add to the stock with the remaining broth ingredients. Strain, cool, then place in the fridge. Skim off the fat on the surface and throw it away. Warm broth, season to taste with salt, pepper, fish sauce and lime, and add noodles and toppings.

Thit heo banh mi

Thit heo simply means 'pork' in Vietnamese and that's just what you get an abundance of in this sandwich, because this is turbo-fuelled with pâté, pork belly and even some crispy crackling if you want.

Makes 4 sandwiches

2 Banh Mi Baguettes (see page 78)
500g/1lb 2oz pork belly
vegetable oil for frying
2 shallots, finely chopped
2 garlic cloves, finely chopped
2 tbsp fish sauce
200ml/7fl oz/scant 1 cup water
2 tbsp palm sugar (or standard granulated)
1 thumb-sized piece fresh ginger, finely grated
1 unripe mango
200g/7oz pork pâté
a bunch of fresh coriander
1–2 bird's eye chillies
Mayonnaise (see page 32)
salt and black pepper
Sriracha sauce

FOR THE QUICK PICKLED CUCUMBER

1 cucumber
4 tbsp granulated sugar
4 tbsp distilled vinegar, 12%
100ml/3½fl oz/scant ½ cup water
½ tsp salt

1. Remove rind from the pork belly. Cut the meat into cubes and fry in oil in a hot frying pan until they've coloured nicely. Take out of the pan and fry the shallots and garlic. Put the meat back in the pan and add fish sauce, water, sugar and grated ginger and grind over a generous amount of black pepper. Season to taste with salt. Lower to medium heat and leave to simmer, covered with a lid, for about 45 minutes, or until it is tender, brown and sticky.

2. Preheat the oven to 220°C/425°F/gas 7. Score the pork rind and pat in a generous amount of salt. Place it on an oven tray and roast in the centre of the oven for 40–50 minutes, or until the rind bubbles up and look crispy. Leave to cool, then cut into thin, small pieces. Cut the mango into matchstick-sized strips.

3. To make the pickled cucumber, slice the cucumber thinly lengthways and put in a bowl. Mix together the sugar, vinegar, water and salt for a quick pickling. Pour it over the cucumber and place in the fridge.

4. Assemble the sandwich – yes! – by scraping out a bit of the crumb and, if the baguettes are cold, crisp them up a bit in the oven. Spread pâté on the bottom half, add cucumber, a ridiculous amount of coriander, mango and then the sticky lovely pork belly. Finish off with finely sliced chilli, mayonnaise, crackling and Sriracha sauce.

VIETNAMESE MEATBALLS

If you don't want pork belly you can always replace it with these lovely meatballs – or you go totally crazy and add them in addition to the pork belly.

SERVES 4

400g/14oz minced pork
4 garlic cloves, finely chopped
3 spring onions, finely chopped
½ pot of basil, chopped
1 tbsp fish sauce
1 tbsp Sriracha sauce (see page 117)
1 tbsp granulated sugar
1 tsp black pepper
1 tsp salt
butter for frying

Preheat the oven to 200°C/400°F/gas 6. Mix together all the ingredients into a classic meatball paste. Shape into balls. Brown off in a frying pan in a little bit of butter, then cook thoroughly in the oven for about 15 minutes. Put the meatballs in the sandwich together with the other ingredients.

Char siu banh mi

Char siu is Chinese for 'grilled pork'. More than that you hardly need to know, right? If you want the characteristic red colour you get in genuine char siu you can always add some red food colouring to the marinade, but I think it's unnecessary.

Makes 6 sandwiches

3 Banh Mi Baguettes (see page 78)
1kg/2lb 4oz pork collar
butter
Sriracha sauce (page 117)
a bunch of fresh coriander
3 jalapeños, finely sliced
spring onion, finely sliced

FOR THE MARINADE

1 tbsp Chinese five-spice
1 tsp white pepper
1½ tbsp granulated sugar
2 tbsp Japanese soy sauce
1 tbsp Chinese soy sauce
1½ tbsp oyster sauce
1½ tbsp black bean paste
4 tbsp clear honey

FOR THE DO CHUA

115g/4oz/½ cup
   granulated sugar
100ml/3½fl oz/scant
   ½ cup distilled vinegar
200ml/7fl oz/1 cup water
1 tsp salt
120g/4¼oz/1 cup
   shredded carrot
120g/4¼oz/1 cup
   shredded daikon (mooli)

1. Preheat the oven to 180°C/350°F/ gas 4. Cut the pork collar into 5cm/2in wide and thick strips. Mix together the ingredients for the marinade and brush over the meat. Don't be stingy. Put the meat in the centre of the oven for 15 minutes. Take it out, brush with more marinade and cook for another 15 minutes, or until the meat is nice and crispy.

2. For the sweet-sour crunch in this sandwich make some Vietnamese pickles, called do chua. Make it at least an hour or maximum a week ahead. Make a brine by heating up the sugar, vinegar, water and salt until everything has dissolved. Leave the brine to cool, then pour over the carrot and daikon, cover with a lid and put in the fridge.

3. Assemble the sandwich by cutting the baguettes in half and scraping out some of the crumb. It's nice to warm them up in the oven for a bit so they get as crispy as possible. Then slice the meat – preferably diagonally. Butter the bread, add a dash of Sriracha sauce, add a dazzlingly large amount of pork and finish off with do chua, coriander and some finely sliced chilli and spring onion.

HOW TO JULIENNE

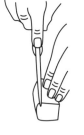

1. Peel the veg and cut into 8cm/3¼in long pieces. Trim off the sides so they get completely square.

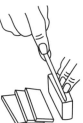

2. Slice the vegetable thinly into 2–4mm/¾–1½in thick slices. Place them in an even pile.

3. Carefully cut the slices lengthways into thin matchsticks. Voilà, you've julienned!

Grilled shrimp po'boy

In New Orleans there's a large community of Vietnamese immigrants, which is said to be the reason for the discernible similarities between the Asian banh mi sandwich and the Southern States' sandwich number one: the po'boy. Love culture mash-up! In this version, inspired by a sandwich from the superb sandwich shop, Killer Po'Boys, the Asian influences are a little more noticeable.

Makes 6 sandwiches

3 Banh Mi Baguettes (see page 78)
6 garlic cloves
Mayonnaise (see page 32)
½ cucumber
600g/1lb 5oz MSC certified raw king prawns
55g/2oz butter
1 tsp Worcestershire sauce
1 tsp Tabasco or other chilli sauce
120g/4¼oz/1 cup grated carrots
120g/4¼oz/1 cup grated fresh daikon (mooli)
a bunch of fresh coriander
a bunch of fresh mint
a bunch of fresh Thai basil
2 bird's eye chillies
squeezed lemon juice
salt and freshly ground black pepper

1. Make a quick aioli by crushing 3 garlic cloves and either stir them into some ready-made mayonnaise or add them to step 1 of the mayo recipe if you make your own. Slice the cucumber thinly lengthways using either a mandolin or potato peeler.
2. Peel the prawns and finely chop the 3 remaining garlic cloves. Melt the butter in a frying pan on medium heat, add the garlic and fry the prawns quickly until they've turned red. Add Worcestershire sauce and Tabasco or chilli sauce and season with lemon juice, salt and pepper to taste.
3. Assemble the sandwich by cutting the baguettes in half and scooping out a little of the crumb. Warm up the bread in the oven for a little bit to make it as crispy as possible. Spread the baguettes with a hell of a lot of aioli, and then add a slice of cucumber on each half. Squeeze in as many prawns as you can fit. Pour over the rest of the garlic butter and add another squeeze of lemon and garnish with carrot, daikon, finely sliced chilli and fresh herbs. Serve with an ice-cold beer.

WATERMELON SALAD

A cooling but hot melon salad is nice together with this – and to pretty much all other sandwiches in this chapter. If you want to save yourself from the spitting, buy a melon without pips.

SERVES 4–6

½ watermelon
3 bird's eye chillies
a bunch of fresh Thai basil
salt

Peel and slice the watermelon into as neat cubes as you possibly can. Slice the bird's eye chillies thinly and mix together with the melon cubes. Tear Thai basil over the top. Season to taste with salt.

Fried oyster po'boy

Originally this classic Louisiana sandwich was called oyster loaf or peacemaker, but when a wildcat strike broke out among New Orleans' tram workers in the 1920s, two pub owners started to hand out free sandwiches to all these 'poor boys' that didn't get their pay cheque. Nowadays oysters aren't at all as affordable any more unfortunately, so there's nothing poor about this sandwich at all.

Makes 2 sandwiches

1 Banh Mi Baguette (see page 78)
oil for deep-frying
20 oysters, preferably as big as possible
200g/7oz/1½ cups cornmeal
60g/2¼oz/½ cup plain flour
2 tsp garlic powder
2 tsp black pepper
½ tsp cayenne pepper
salt
40 Thousand Billion Island Sauce (see page 32)
1 tomato, sliced
Dill Pickles (see page 113)
½ head iceberg lettuce, shredded
freshly squeezed lemon juice
Chilli Sauce (see page 124)

1. Heat the oil to 180°C/350°F and open the oysters. Mix together the cornmeal with the flour, garlic powder, black pepper cayenne and some salt. Dip the oysters in the flour mixture and deep-fry quickly until golden brown, about 2 minutes. Leave to drain on a piece of kitchen paper.

2. Assemble the sandwich by cutting the baguettes in half and scraping out some of the crumb. Warm the bread in the oven for a bit so it gets as crispy as possible. Spread some 40 thousand billion island sauce on the bread. Add the sliced tomatoes and dill pickles along the edge, stuff with shredded lettuce and then with the freshly fried oysters. Finish off with a squeeze of lemon juice, chilli sauce and more 40 thousand billion island sauce. Eat immediately.

HOW TO OPEN OYSTERS

1. *Place the oyster with the rounded-side down and localise the 'hinge' at the pointy end of the oyster. It's a good idea to hold the oyster with a tea towel so you don't slip with the knife.*

2. *Push in the oyster knife into the 'hinge' and use a twisting motion until the shell starts to open. Push the knife further into the oyster.*

3. *Run the knife all along the oyster to ensure it's fully open.*

4. *Remove the shell. Carefully cut the oyster away from the bottom shell. Remove any grit and bits of shell.*

Torta ahogada

Torta ahogada means 'drowned sandwich', which in this case means that it's served standing up in a bowl of salsa – it goes incredibly well with this chewy, crispy baguette bread. Torta ahogada is a speciality from the Mexican state Jalisco, and the meat that we use is carnitas in its simplest and most classic form – just crispy, wonderful, thready pork collar.

Makes 4 sandwiches

2 Banh Mi Baguettes
   (page 78)
Refried Beans (page 131)
Pickled Red Onion
   (page 112)
1 white onion, sliced
a bunch of fresh coriander

FOR THE CARNITAS

1kg/2lb 4oz pork collar
225g/8oz lard
1.5 litres/2½ pints/
   6½ cups water
1 tbsp salt

FOR THE SALSA

1 brown onion, quartered
4 tomatoes, quartered
6 garlic cloves
2–4 dried chillies, such as
   ancho or chile de árbol,
   deseeded
100–200ml/3½–7fl oz/
   scant ½–generous ¾
   cup chicken stock
½ bunch of fresh
   coriander
2 tsp white wine vinegar
salt

1. Dice the pork collar and bring to the boil together with lard, water and salt in a cast-iron pan. Lower to a medium heat, cover and simmer gently for 45 minutes. Remove the lid and continue to simmer until all the water has reduced off and the pork starts to fry crispy in the fat. When it's at its crispiest but before it gets dry, remove the meat from the heat.

2. While the meat is cooking, prepare the refried beans and pickled onion.

3. To make the salsa, boil the onion and tomatoes together with the garlic and chilli in enough stock to just cover, for about 15 minutes. Leave to cool. Blend everything until smooth together with the coriander and vinegar. Sieve and add salt to taste.

4. Assemble the sandwich by cutting the baguettes in half and scraping out some of the crumb. Spread them with beans, add the meat and put them in the oven until the bread is crispy. Add the red onion, sliced white onion and coriander. Pour the hot salsa in a bowl and stand the sandwiches upright in it for maximum effect. Or you can serve the salsa in little pots on the side.

THE WORLD'S MOST WIDESPREAD CHILLI SAUCE

Nowadays, when there are thousands of chilli sauces to choose from, we ought not to forget the original: Tabasco. Tabasco was invented in Louisiana in 1868 by the banker Edmund McIlheny, who in the beginning re-used old perfume bottles for packaging the chilli sauce – a shape that the bottle still remains in today. In 1890 his son John Avery took over the business but soon quit to join Theodore Roosevelt's cavalry regiment, Rough Riders. This guy Edmund's second son, Edward – who was a nudist and Arctic explorer – then took over the business and made the company into one of those iconic brands. Still today both the salt and the chillies in the sauce come from Louisiana's Avery Island, where they are also fermented for three years in old Jack Daniels' casks. There's always a bottle of Tabasco on Air Force One for the president, all American soldiers have a mini bottle in their emergency rations and it's the only chilli sauce that's been into space.

Pepito torta

Torta simply means 'sandwich' in Mexican. This one in particular is filled with pickled chilli, tomatillo salsa, cheese, fried onion, avocado, beans and braised short ribs cooked for so long they fall apart just by looking at them.

Makes 6 sandwiches

3 Banh Mi Baguettes (see page 78)

1.5kg/3lb 5oz thin rib or chuck

3 garlic cloves, chopped

5 brown onions

1 tbsp Worcestershire sauce

1 tbsp Japanese soy sauce

500ml/17fl oz/generous 2 cups beef stock

1 batch Refried Beans (see page 131)

350g/12oz/3 cups grated Swiss cheese, such as Gruyère or Comté

Pickled Chilli (see page 113)

3 avocados

olive oil for frying

salt

FOR THE SALSA

6 tomatillos

2 white onions

3 garlic cloves

½ bunch of fresh coriander

2 tbsp corn oil

1–2 chillies, such as jalapeño, pickled (see page 113)

1. Trim the sinews and fat off the thin rib, cut into cubes and sprinkle with salt. Heat up the oil in a heavy-based pan and brown off in batches. Chop the garlic and 2 of the onions and add. Make sure to save all the good meat juices. Add the Worcestershire sauce, soy sauce and stock and braise on a low heat for about 3–4 hours, covered with a lid, until the meat is almost falling apart.

2. While the meat is simmering away you can start with the tomatillo salsa. Preheat the oven to maximum and oven-roast the tomatillo, white onion, garlic and jalapeño until coloured, without adding any oil. Blend until smooth. Add the coriander and blend a little more. Season to taste with salt. Leave to cool. And don't forget to pickle the jalapeño if you haven't done so already.

3. Slice the remaining onions thinly and fry in a little oil over a medium heat for about 15 minutes. Lower the heat, add salt and pour over some gravy from the meat and leave to caramelise for a further 30 minutes. When the meat is ready, pull it apart a little with two forks and mix into the tasty braising juices. But not too much; you've got teeth and know how to use them, right?

4. Assemble the sandwich by cutting the baguettes in half and scraping out some of the crumb. Spread with refried beans, add meat and some grated cheese and put in the oven until the cheese has melted and the bread has turned crispy. Add onion, sliced avocado and pickled jalapeño. Pour over some of the salsa and serve the rest on the side for dipping.

French dip

Except for the fact that this is served 'au jus' – with gravy for dipping – it doesn't have much to do with France. Instead it's an American invention, which several pubs in California all claim to have come up with first. In any case, the French dip is one of those sandwiches which is so much greater than the sum of its parts.

Makes 4 sandwiches

2 Banh Mi Baguettes (see page 78)
about 1.5kg/3lb 5oz roast beef, whole
salt and freshly ground black pepper
Dijon mustard
fresh horseradish
oil for frying
butter

FOR THE AU JUS

2 shallots, finely chopped
55g/2oz butter, plus extra for frying
300ml/10½fl oz/generous 1¼ cups red wine
1 fresh rosemary sprig
1 bay leaf
the gravy from the meat
salt and freshly ground black pepper

1. Even if you might not eat this quantity of meat in one sitting, it's good if you can avoid buying a beef-roasting joint that's too small. The bigger ones are juicier and tastier, and it's awesome to have some extra sandwich fillings. Or, think the other way around – make a Sunday roast and then eat the leftovers as the world's coolest lunch sandwich.

2. In any case, preheat the oven to 100°C/225°C/gas ¼. Brown off the meat in oil in a hot frying pan. Sprinkle with salt and pepper, and put into a snug-fitting oven dish. Roast in the oven until the inside temperature has reached 55°C/131°F, which usually takes about 2–3 hours. The meat should be nice and pink. Leave it to cool and then wrap in kitchen foil and put in the fridge. Pour about 200ml/7fl oz/scant 1 cup water in the oven dish and scrape off all the good bits. Save the gravy.

3. Make your 'au jus' by frying the shallots in a knob of butter in a saucepan over a medium heat until transparent. Add the wine, rosemary and bay leaf and leave to simmer until reduced by half. Pour in the roast gravy and reduce to half one more time. Season to taste with salt and pepper. Sieve, then return the gravy to the hob and stir in the butter so it's shiny and lovely.

4. Now assemble the sandwiches. Remove some of the crumb from the baguettes and warm them up in the oven until crispy. Spread with a generous amount of butter and add an even more generous amount of thinly sliced roast beef. Grate over lots of horseradish and serve with Dijon mustard and the warm gravy in a bowl on the side.

OTHER FAMOUS VARIETIES

TEXAS DIP
Replace the roast beef with smoked brisket.

FRENCH CHEESE DIP
Add melted Swiss cheese, such as Comté.

TURKEY DIP
Replace the roast beef with thinly sliced turkey breast.

BEEF ON WECK
Replace the baguettes with kummelweck, a German bun with fennel seeds.

FROM SCRATCH: SMOKED BACON

1kg/2lb 4oz pork belly
2 tbsp salt
1 tbsp curing salt (can
   be replaced with
   normal cooking salt
   (see page 52)
3½ tbsp brown sugar
apple wood smoking
   chips

CLASSIC SMOKED BACON Few things beat having a beautiful piece of home-smoked bacon in the fridge that's just waiting there for you to take it out, slice it up and fry it.

1. Trim your pork belly so it looks appealing. It's a good idea to remove those flaps that remain from where the ribs used to sit but leave the rind on. Mix together the salt, curing salt and sugar and rub it into the pork belly. Wrap the meat in a double layer of plastic bags and leave in the fridge for 7 days. Turn it over once a day.
2. Rinse the pork belly thoroughly and leave to dry on a rack in the fridge for 1 more day.
3. Prepare your smoker and heat it to about 95°C/203°F. Throw in a couple of handfuls of wood smoking chips and smoke the bacon for about 2–3 hours until the inside temperature has reached 65°C/149°F. Leave to cool. You've now got bacon!
4. Remove but save the rind – it's perfect to throw in as a flavour enhancer when you cook soup or beans. Slice your bacon thinly and fry until crispy.

1kg/2lb 4oz pork shoulder
   with rind
2 tbsp salt
1 tbsp curing salt, or
   can be replaced with
   normal cooking salt
   (see page 52)
3½ tbsp brown sugar
1 tbsp black pepper
1 tsp fennel seeds
2 garlic cloves
apple wood smoking
   chips

PORK SHOULDER BACON You'll get a bacon that's a bit more substantial with less fat and more lean meat if you use pork shoulder instead of pork belly.

1. Mix together the spices for the dry curing and rub into the pork shoulder. Crush the garlic cloves and throw in with the pork. Wrap the meat in a double layer of plastic bags and leave in the fridge for 7 days so that the liquid gets drawn out and the meat gets firm and nice. Turn it over once a day.
2. Rinse the pork shoulder thoroughly and leave to dry on a rack in the fridge for 1 more day.
3. Prepare your smoker and heat it to about 95°C/203°F. Throw in a couple of handfuls of wood smoking chips and smoke the bacon for about 2–3 hours, until the inside temperature has reached 65°C/150°F. Leave to cool.
4. As above, remove but save the rind.

FROM SCRATCH: FRESH BACON

1 pork cheek
2 tbsp salt
2 tsp granulated sugar
½ tsp dried coriander
1 tsp black pepper
1 tsp curing salt (can be replaced with normal cooking salt (see page 52)
1 fresh rosemary sprig
1 garlic clove, crushed

PORK CHEEK BACON This quick version of the Italian guanciale is truly the Rolls Royce of bacon. The cheek might well be the fattiest part of the pig and is perfectly for making into bacon, so what are you waiting for?

1. Mix together the dry ingredients and pat into the meat. Place the cheek, the rosemary sprig and the crushed garlic in a plastic bag — or two for that matter to make sure it won't leak any pork juice. Leave to dry cure in the fridge for 3 days.
2. Preheat the oven to 120°C/250°F/gas ½. Rinse and dry the pork cheek thoroughly. Roast in the centre of the oven 2½ hours.
3. When it's time to make a bacon sandwich, you just slice the pork cheek thinly and fry crispy in a frying pan.

1kg/2lb 4oz pork belly
2 tbsp salt
1 tbsp curing salt,
   or can be replaced
   with normal cooking
   salt (see page 52)
 3½ tbsp brown sugar
2 garlic cloves
1 tbsp black pepper
1 tsp crushed coriander
   seeds
2 bay leaves
1 fresh thyme sprig

PANCETTA A quick version of the Italian dried bacon. Fry crispy to serve.

1. Remove the rind from the pork belly and trim off those flaps that remain from where the ribs used to sit. The rind you can save and make into Chicharones (see page 150).
2. Mix together the dry ingredients and pat into the pork belly. Place it with the thyme sprig and the crushed garlic clove in double plastic bags. Leave to dry-cure in the fridge for 7 days in the fridge, turning over once a day.
3. Rinse and dry the pork belly thoroughly. Then roll it together as tightly as you possible can and tie together with kitchen string. Hang up to dry on a suitable place in the fridge for 7 days. You've now got pancetta!

Sicilian

LOAF

This simple bread is traditionally used for New Orleans' sandwich pride — the muffuletta, and could be described as an Americanised version of the focaccia — but baked in a round tin instead of a square, and without all those olives and dried tomatoes pushed into the bread. It's just amazingly oily and fantastically soft with a crispy crust.

Sicilian loaf

The word muffuletta is a regional Sicilian word for a large, round variety of bread and that's just why we bake it in a round tin. You should be able to get hold of the tin in most cookery shops. The downside with baking it in this tin is that the bottom can get soggy instead of lovely and crispy, but if that happens all you have to do is to take the bread out of the tin and bake it upside-down in the oven for another 5 minutes.

Makes 2 round breads

2 tsp fast-action dried
   yeast
400ml/14fl oz/1¾ cups
   tepid water
670g/1lb 7½oz/4¼ cups
   strong white bread
   flour, plus extra for
   dusting
2 tsp salt
3 tbsp olive oil, plus extra
   for greasing
sea salt
sesame seeds

1. Mix together the dried yeast and water directly in the dough mixer bowl. Add the flour, salt and 2 tbsp olive oil and run for 2 minutes, or until the dough is smooth and nice. Shape the dough into a ball, put back into the bowl, cover with clingfilm and leave to rise for about 2 hours until doubled in size.

2. Turn out the dough on a floured worktop, flatten it out a little and divide into two equally sized halves. Shape into balls and place them in two 20cm/8in round tins that you've greased with a little oil. Push the dough down a little so it covers the whole tin. If you haven't got a tin, you can freestyle a round ball shape and place on an oven tray. Pour 1 tsp oil over each dough, cover with clingfilm and leave to rise for another 40 minutes. Preheat the oven to 220°C/425°F/gas 7.

3. Sprinkle the breads with sea salt and sesame seeds. Place in the centre of the oven and turn immediately down to 190°C/375°F/gas 5. Bake for 20–25 minutes or until the bread is golden brown. Take out and leave to cool. Depending on what kind of tin you have, the bottom can sometimes get a bit soggy. In which case, bake it for another 5 minutes. No problem.

NEW ORLEANS' THREE BEST MUFFULETTAS

CENTRAL GROCERY
923 Decatur Street
The place that invented this classic sandwich is tiny and always has a super-long queue – be prepared to know what to order.

COCHON BUTCHER
930 Tchoupitoulas Street
(www.cochonbutcher.com)
A more modern variety of the muffuletta. All cold cuts are made in the shop and they also serve the sandwich hot, so the melted cheese factor is considerably higher.

ZEPHYR FIELD
6000 Airline Drive
The muffuletta at this sports stadium might not be the third best in New Orleans, but in combination with an ice-cold Dixie and thousands of screaming baseball fans, it's a fantastic experience.

THE SANDWICH LOVER'S GUIDE TO CHARCUTERIE

1. *Prosciutto cotto.* Not all Italian hams are dry cured. In fact, I think this boiled Italian variety is often better suited to sandwiches than the chewy flavour-rich solo artist Parma ham.

2. *Mortadella.* Classic Italian sandwich filler. Bigger, softer and cosier than Totoro.
3. *Sopressa.* The perfect sandwich salami. Good texture, not too overpowering in flavour.

4. *Pancetta.* When I haven't got time to make my own but still fancy a bit of quality bacon I always go for a proper bit of pancetta to slice thinly and fry crispy.

5. *Guanciale.* Italian dried pork cheek. The Rolls Royce of bacon.

Muffuletta

This classic sandwich was invented at Central Grocery right in the centre of New Orleans' beautiful French Quarter. Italian workers would come in and order cold cuts as well as Sicilian muffuletta bread that they would then eat sitting down, with all the food balanced on their laps. Some bright person then came up with the idea that it would be a whole lot easier if you stuffed the sausage, cheese and ham into the bread and — just like that —one of the word's most iconic sandwiches was born.

Serves 1–4

1 Sicilian loaf (see page 102)
100g/3½oz Italian salami, such as sopressa
150g/5oz provolone cheese
100g/3½oz mortadella

FOR THE GIARDINIERA

about 200g/7oz cauliflower florets
1 small carrot
1 small celery stick
1 tbsp extra virgin olive oil
½ tsp dried oregano
½ tsp dried thyme
3 tbsp water
100g/3½oz/¾ cup green olives
50g/1¾oz/½ cup black olives
2 tbsp pickled red chillis
1 tbsp finely chopped fresh parsley
1 tbsp red wine vinegar
salt and freshly ground black pepper

1. To make the giardiniera, finely chop cauliflower, carrot and celery and place in a pan with oil, oregano, thyme and water. Simmer over a medium heat until the vegetables have just softened, about 10 minutes. Leave to cool. Finely chop olives and chilli and mix together with the other vegetables and the parsley. Add the vinegar and season to taste with salt and pepper. Leave to one side.

2. Cut the top off your Sicilian loaf as if it was a lid and then scrape out quite a lot of the crumb from the bottom – it should be a big hole, enough to stuff with ridiculous amounts of filling, but not so big that just the crust remains. But you're an adult so you can probably judge for yourself. In any case, cover the bottom with a couple of tablespoons of your giardiniera, and then get started on the layering. Place a layer of sopressa in the sandwich first, then a layer of provolone and finally a layer of mortadella. It's important that nothing pokes out of the hole. Repeat in the same order until the muffuletta is full. Finish off with a

layer of giardiniera on the inside of the lid, too.

3. Now it's time to press this sandwich together into one yummy unity. Do this by placing it back into the tin, cover with a piece of greaseproof paper, then place a plate on top and finally, a weight. Leave in the fridge for 2 hours.

4. When it's time to eat, preheat the oven to 150°C/300°F/gas 2, and start by warming the muffuletta in the oven for 5–10 minutes, while you make up your mind about how many people can share it with you. Tough nuts eat the whole thing themselves, of course. Hungry people eat half and normal people eat a quarter. So divide the sandwich into whatever number you decide on and enjoy.

Pan bagnat

When you prepare this sandwich, make sure not to be stingy on the olive oil, pan bagnat literally means 'bathed bread'. This old picnic favourite tastes of the French Riviera, and that's not so strange – a pan bagnat is simply a salad Niçoise in a practical bread packaging. Don't slice the sandwich up until it's time to eat. Then you won't have to deal with any mess.

Serves 4

1 Sicilian loaf (see page 102)
1 tomato
1 egg
200g/7oz can of tuna in oil, drained
½ red onion, sliced
a bunch of fresh basil
6 anchovies
50g/1¾oz/½ cup chopped black olives
2 tbsp capers
olive oil
red wine vinegar
salt and freshly ground black pepper

1. Cut the top off your Sicilian loaf as if it was a lid and then scrape out quite a lot of the crumb from the bottom. The hole should be big enough to stuff with filling but no so big so only the crust remains. Slice the tomato and place in the bottom. Then add layers of sliced egg, tuna, onion, basil, anchovy, olives and capers. Drizzle over some oil and vinegar, then season with salt and pepper.

2. Now it's time to press this sandwich together into one yummy unity. Do this by placing it back in the tin, cover with a piece of greaseproof paper, then place a plate on top and finally, a weight. Leave in the fridge for 1–2 hours, or until it's time to set off for the picnic.

3. When it's time to eat you just have to take out the sandwich from the tin, slice it into four pieces and enjoy it on a blanket with the sun in your face.

»Death is the sound of distant thunder at a picnic.«
– *W. H. Auden*

Eggplant parm

Parm is in this case an abbreviation of parmigiana, a Sicilian vegetable dish that's become a symbol for simple Italian cuisine in New York, particularly in Little Italy. If you want to make variations on your classic aubergine parm, you can just as well use chicken, as in the recipe below, or even use the meatballs as on page 138.

Serves 4

1 Sicilian loaf (page 102)
2 aubergines
2 eggs
3 tbsp grated Parmesan
　cheese
3 tbsp grated pecorino
　cheese
100g/3½oz/2 cups panko
　breadcrumbs
1 ball of Mozzarella (see
　page 72)
a bunch of fresh basil
olive oil for frying
vegetable oil,
　for deep-frying

FOR THE SAUCE

150ml/5fl oz/scant ⅔ cup
　olive oil
½ onion, finely chopped
4 garlic cloves, finely
　chopped
½ tsp chilli flakes
½ tbsp tomato purée
1 tsp dried oregano
1 bay leaf
½ tsp granulated sugar
400g/14oz can of whole
　tomatoes
salt and black pepper

1. Start by making the tomato sauce. Heat 4 tbsp of the oil in a saucepan over a medium heat and fry the onion and garlic until they start to soften. Add the chilli flakes, tomato purée, oregano, bay leaf, sugar, tomatoes, salt and pepper and leave to simmer for about 1 hour. Stir occasionally.

2. Peel the aubergine and cut it into about 1cm/½in thick slices. Sprinkle with salt on both sides and leave for 10 minutes. Rinse and pat dry, then fry them in a little olive oil in a frying pan over medium heat until soft.

3. Heat the deep-frying oil to 180°C/350°F. Stir together egg, Parmesan and pecorino and pour into a bowl. Dip the aubergine in the egg mixture first, then into the panko, then deep-fry until golden. Leave to drain on a piece of kitchen paper.

4. Cut the top off your Sicilian loaf and then scrape out quite a lot of the crumb from the bottom. Fill with a layer of aubergine, then a generous dollop of tomato sauce and a few basil leaves. Finish off with a layer of thinly sliced mozzarella. Put the lid on top and warm in the oven at 150°C/300°F/gas 2 for about 10 minutes. Cut into quarters and eat.

CHICKEN PARM

For a chicken parm, follow all steps in the recipe to the left but replace the aubergine with fried chicken.

SERVES 4

*4 chicken breasts,
about 150g/5oz each
100g/3½oz/2 cups plain flour
2 tsp chilli powder
2 tsp cumin
1 tbsp paprika
1 tsp salt
1 egg
200g/7 oz/4 cups panko
oil for deep-frying*

Butterfly the chicken breast by slicing it sideways until the knife has almost cut through the meat and then fold it out like a book. Bash it with a meat tenderiser or a pan or other implement so that you get a large 1cm/½in thick chicken breast.

Heat the deep-frying oil to around 160°C/325°F (or until a bit of panko sizzles nicely). Mix together the flour and spices on a plate, place the beaten egg on another and the panko on a third. Dip the fillets in the spiced flour first, then in the egg and finally in the panko. Deep-fry the chicken until golden and crispy. Leave to drain on kitchen paper.

Pickled Egg.

Pickled Okra.

Dill Pickles.

Quick Pickled
Cucumber.

Pickled Red Onion.

FROM SCRATCH: PICKLES

PICKLED RED ONION Beautifully red with a lovely sweet-sour crunch, pickled red onion is a must for every serious sandwich lover.

3 red onions, thinly sliced
250ml/9fl oz/generous 1 cup distilled vinegar
250ml/9fl oz/generous 1 cup water
250g/9oz/heaped 1 cup granulated sugar
1 tbsp salt
½ tsp whole allspice
½ tsp mustard seeds
2 bay leaves

Sterilise a pickle jar in boiling water or in the oven at 110°C/225°F/gas ¼ for 10 minutes. Add the onion. Bring the rest of the ingredients to the boil and simmer until the sugar has dissolved. Pour over the onion. Leave overnight to get the right pink colour.

PICKLED OKRA Okra will get super-spicy and (almost) not at all slimy if you pickle it. Good as a snack and palate cleanser.

250g/9oz okra, stalks trimmed
½ lemon
3 tsp coriander seeds
3 tsp chilli flakes
1 tsp fennel seeds
1 tsp black peppercorns
1 tsp mustard seeds
2 garlic cloves

250ml/9fl oz/generous 1 cup apple cider vinegar
250ml/9fl oz/generous 1 cup water
1 tbsp salt
2 tsp granulated sugar

Sterilise a pickle jar in boiling water or in the oven at 110°C/225°F/gas ¼ for 10 minutes. Place a slice of lemon in the bottom of the jar. Add the dried spices, the okra and slightly crushed garlic cloves. Bring the vinegar, water, salt and sugar to the boil and simmer until salt and sugar have dissolved, then pour over the okra. Put the lid on and store in the fridge. It will keep fresh for at least a month.

PICKLED EGG This classic bar snack is also beautiful to slice and serve on your sandwich.

6 eggs
½ tsp whole allspice
½ tsp mustard seeds
1 tsp black peppercorns
2 bay leaves
250ml/9fl oz/generous 1 cup beetroot brine
200ml/7fl oz/scant 1 cup apple cider vinegar
4 tbsp granulated sugar

Hard-boil and shell the eggs. Sterilise a pickle jar in boiling water or in the oven at 110°C/225°F/gas ¼ for 10 minutes. Add the dried spices and the eggs. Mix together beetroot brine, vinegar and sugar and stir until the sugar has dissolved, then pour over the eggs. Leave in the fridge overnight at least until the eggs have coloured.

PICKLED CHILLI
Perfect both as a snack and as a sandwich filler. If you can, leave them in the fridge for at least a week before digging in.

250g/9oz jalapeños
300ml/10½fl oz/1¼ cups water
300ml/10½fl oz/1¼ cups white wine vinegar
1½ tbsp granulated sugar
1½ tbsp salt
1 bay leaf
1 tbsp coriander seeds
2 garlic cloves
1 tbsp black peppercorns

Hard-boil and shell the eggs. Sterilise a pickle jar in boiling water or in the oven at 110°C/225°F/gas ¼ for 10 minutes. Add the chillies. Bring the rest of the ingredients to the boil, then pour over. Cover with a lid and leave to stand for a week before you start eating them.

DILL PICKLES
This classic deli pickle gets its characteristic flavour from both dill flowers and a slight fermentation.

10 pickling cucumbers
2 litres/3½ pints/8½ cups water
3 tbsp salt without added iodine
3 tsp coriander seeds
3 tsp chilli flakes
1 tsp fennel seeds
1 tsp black peppercorns
1 tsp mustard seeds
4 garlic cloves, peeled
3 bay leaves
a bunch of dill flowers

Bring the water, salt and dried spices to the boil. Sterilise a couple of jars in boiling water or in the oven at 110°C/225°F/gas ¼ for 10 minutes. Pack the cucumbers tightly in one, or more, jars with the garlic cloves and the dill. Pour over the brine and cover with a tea towel to protect it from dirt but let air in. Leave to stand at room temperature for 2-6 days to ferment, it depends a bit on how sour you'd like your gherkins. When they taste nice, cover with a lid and put it in the fridge.

QUICK PICKLED CUCUMBER
Need pickled cucumber for your sandwiches? NOW!? If so, make this super-speedy pickle.

1 cucumber
1 tbsp distilled vinegar
100ml/3½fl oz/scant ½ cup water
2 tbsp granulated sugar
salt and freshly ground black pepper

Peel and julienne the cucumber (see page 84). Don't bother with the watery bit in the centre. Mix together the vinegar, water and sugar and season to taste with salt and black pepper. Pour the brine over cucumber and, hey presto, it's pickled!

Steamed

BUNS

Gua bao has been Taiwan's most popular fast food for decades, but it wasn't until the chef David Chang put a version of it on the menu of his New York restaurant a couple a years ago that the cute little sandwich started to become known in wider circles. Nowadays these soft, cosy steamed buns can be filled with lots of different things, a little bit like an Asian taco. I'd recommended, however, that you start with one of the fillings that follow before you begin experimenting yourself.

Steamed buns

Bao (or bau, pow or baozi) is the Chinese word for 'steamed bread', and that's exactly what these strange little white Kermit faces are. This recipe originates from David Chang – even though I've modified it slightly. 30 baos might sound like a lot, but they will get eaten, and if not they freeze very well. Just defrost in the steamer when it's time to eat.

Makes 30 buns

12g/½oz fast-action
    dried yeast
350ml/12fl oz/1½ cups
    tepid water
600g/1lb 5oz/4¾ cups
    strong white bread
    flour
6 tbsp granulated sugar
3 tbsp powdered milk
1 tbsp salt
½ tsp bicarbonate of soda
½ tsp baking powder
100g/3½oz butter, at
    room temperature

1. Mix together the yeast and water directly in the dough mixer bowl and then add the flour, sugar, powdered milk, salt, bicarbonate of soda and baking powder. Start the dough mixer and add the butter, one dollop at a time until it's all mixed in. Run on the lowest setting for about 10 minutes. You can also knead the dough by hand, but it will take about double the time. Cover with clingfilm and leave to rise for 1¼ hours.

2. Divide the dough into 30 pieces and shape into ping-pong sized balls. If the dough is too sticky you can sprinkle some flour over the worktop, but normally you won't have to. Cover with a tea towel and leave to rise for another 30 minutes. Meanwhile, cut out 30 pieces of baking parchment each measuring 5cm/1¾in square. Roll out the dough balls into small ovals, fold them in half and put them on a piece of baking parchment. Leave to rise for another 30 minutes.

3. Bring water to the boil in a pan fitted with a steamer (if you haven't got one you can find cheap bamboo steamers in Asian food stores) and steam for 10–15 minutes. Place the steamer on the table and let people assemble their own baos.

HOW TO FOLD THE DOUGH

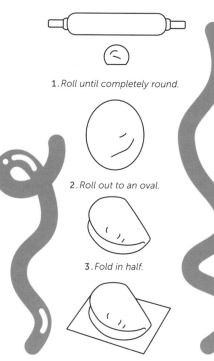

1. *Roll until completely round.*

2. *Roll out to an oval.*

3. *Fold in half.*

4. *Place on a piece of baking parchment.*

THE SANDWICH LOVER'S GUIDE TO THE ASIAN FOOD STORE

1. *Mexican or long coriander.* For a milder flavour and more crunch, this is a good alternative to standard coriander.
2. *Kewpie mayonnaise.* Record-breakingly creamy, umami-packed Japanese mayonnaise that's so popular in its home country that its fans are called 'mayonaras'.
3. *Sriracha sauce.* An umami-packed American (really) chilli sauce of Thai model that's got a just as ardent following as the Kewpie mayonnaise.
4. *Bird's eye chilli.* Hotter and cheaper than red or green chilli.
5. *Unripe papaya (or mango).* Less sweet and firmer than ripe fruit and therefore perfect for beautifully julienned slaw and all kinds of salsa.
6. *Pickled mustard.* Also called pak ghar or collard mustard, this is the traditional condiment for gua bao.
7. *Kimchi.* If you can't face making your own, the kind of kimchi that you find in the fridge in Asian food stores will be a much better alternative to the tinned version you'll find in supermarkets.

Gua bao. ———

Pork buns.

Pork buns

The absolute most common filling in a bao is, of course, oven-roasted pork belly. The reason is very simple: it's fricking tasty. Below follows two versions of these so-called pork buns, firstly the traditional Taiwanese gua bao, and secondly David Chang's Peking-duck-influenced Momofuku pork buns. But you don't have to ponder about which one seems the tastiest, as the garnishes are so easy to do that you can try both.

Serves 6

1 batch Steamed Buns
   (see page 116)
2kg/4lb 8oz pork belly,
   diced
3½ tbsp salt
3½ tbsp granulated sugar

GARNISHES FOR

GUA BAO

salted peanuts
Pickled Mustard (see
   page 117)
Mexican coriander or
   ordinary coriander
Sriracha sauce (see
   page 117)

GARNISHES FOR

PORK BUNS

Mexican coriander or
   ordinary coriander
spring onions
1 cucumber
1 tsp salt
1 tsp granulated sugar
hoisin sauce

1. If you want to munch down on a pork bun you will have to have to do some forward planning and start the preparations one day ahead. However, this is not very difficult; just remove the rind from the pork belly with a sharp, thin knife and then trim off the meat where the ribs were joined so that you get a neat and completely square piece of pork. Pat equal amounts of salt and sugar into the meat, wrap it in clingfilm and leave the meat to cure in the fridge overnight.

2. The next day, preheat the oven to 220°C/425°F/gas 7 for a while before you want to start cooking your meat. Rinse off the salt and sugar mixture, pat the meat dry, place the pork belly in an oven dish and roast in the oven for 1 hour. Lower the heat to 120°C/250°F/gas ½ and roast for another 1¼ hours. Take out the pork belly, taste a little and then leave to cool until completely cold so you can slice it into nice pieces.

3. Before serving, slice the meat and put in the oven for a bit to reheat. Prepare the garnishes for the traditional gua bao by blending the peanuts to a fine powder; rinse, slice and fry the pickled mustard and put this and the finely chopped Mexican coriander in bowls. Put the Sriracha sauce on the table. The same thing for the pork buns: slice the cucumber thinly and pour over equal amounts of salt and sugar for a quick pickling, and put finely chopped Mexican coriander and spring onion in bowls. Pour out hoisin sauce into a bowl. Put the steamed buns and the meat out on the table, show your guests how to assemble the different sandwiches and then let them make their own baos, as if you were having a super-cool taco party or something. Fantastic!

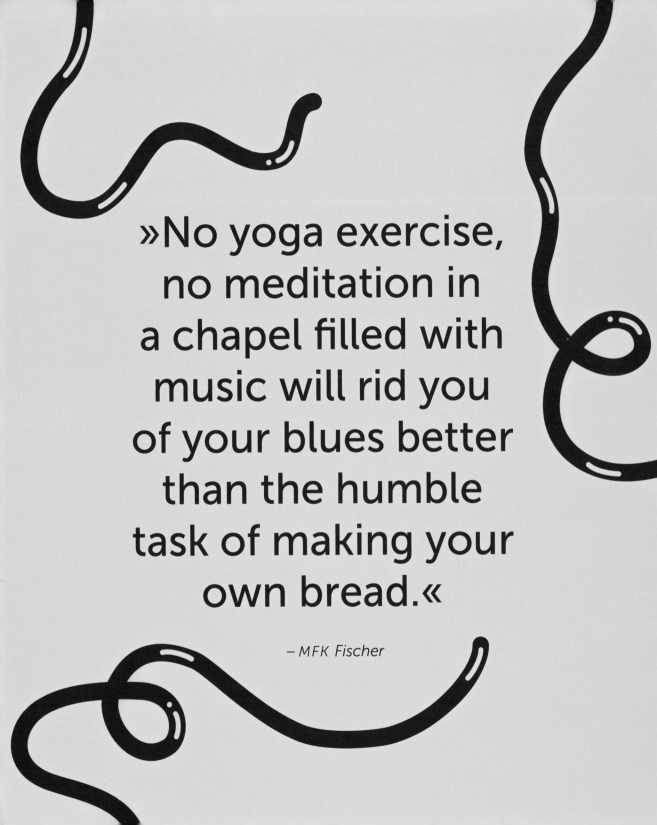

»No yoga exercise, no meditation in a chapel filled with music will rid you of your blues better than the humble task of making your own bread.«

– MFK Fischer

Bulgogi bao

Bulgogi is a delicious Korean grill dish, but it becomes even better served in a bao. Just make sure to buy good-quality meat, which you slice really thinly. Yes, you could even ask your butcher to slice it for you in their super-cool slicing machine. The kimchi you can make yourself or buy from the fridge in an Asian food store.

Serves 4

**1 batch Steamed Buns
(see page 116)**

FOR THE BULGOGI

500g/1lb 2oz rib eye steak
**4 garlic cloves,
finely chopped**
**2 spring onions,
finely sliced**
3 tbsp Japanese soy
2 tbsp granulated sugar
2 tbsp mirin
1 tbsp sesame oil
**1 tsp freshly ground
black pepper**
2 tsp sesame seeds
oil for deep-frying

FOR THE GARNISHES

**Quick Pickled Cucumber
(see page 113)**
kimchi
**ssamjang or Sriracha
sauce (see page 117)**
toasted sesame seeds

1. To make the rib eye easier to slice, put it in the freezer for 1 hour and then slice it as thinly as you possibly can against the meat grain, preferably about 3mm/⅛ in thick.
2. Start with the marinade. Mix together the garlic, spring onions, soy sauce, sugar, mirin, sesame oil, pepper and sesame seeds. Mix the meat together with the marinade and leave to stand in the fridge for 1 hour.
3. Meanwhile, quickly pickle the cucumber by julienning it nicely, dissolving sugar and salt in water and vinegar and pour over. Fry the kimchi in a little oil in a frying pan over a medium heat for about 5 minutes.
4. Hot and quick are the key things when frying bulgogi, so heat a cast-iron pan with a little oil in it to maximum temperature. Shake off the marinade as best as you can and place the meat in one layer on the pan. Fry quickly in batches until it gets beautifully caramelised and smells heavenly.
5. Assemble the bao by squirting the bread with ssamjang or Sriracha sauce, add some kimchi, pickled cucumber and loads of bulgogi and garnish with extra sesame seeds.

KALBI BAO

The other famous Korean grill dish is, that's right, kalbi, which is marinated, thinly sliced ribs of beef, so called short ribs or thin ribs. If your local butcher doesn't have any kalbi, ask him to slice beef ribs about 5cm/1¾in thick and across.

SERVES 4

500g/1lb 2oz kalbi

For the kalbi marinade
100ml/3½fl oz/scant ½ cup Korean
or Japanese soy sauce
3½ tbsp beer (water will work too)
2 tbsp sesame oil
2 tbsp rice vinegar
2 tbsp granulated sugar
1–2 tbsp finely chopped garlic
1 tbsp Sriracha sauce
(see page 117)
3 tbsp grated fresh ginger root
a few tbsp thinly sliced spring onion

Mix together the ingredients for the marinade, add the meat and leave to stand in the fridge for at least 1 hour. Follow the instructions for bulgogi for cooking the meat and preparing the garnishes, but if your kalbi comes on the bone, cut if off before putting it in your bao, of course.

Crispy prawn bao

Now, while we're at stuffing things in a bao bread, we might just as well ignore the authenticity police completely and stuff in a deep-fried prawn – it's so delicious. Just make sure to buy prawns from a sustainable source. Nothing is quite this tasty. Miso is an umami packed Japanese flavour enhancer which, when mixed together with mayonnaise, is so tasty it will broaden your senses.

Serves 6

1 batch Steamed Buns (see page 116)
500g/1lb 2oz fresh prawns
125g/4½oz/1 cup plain flour
2 tsp salt
2 eggs
3 tbsp milk
100g/3½oz/2 cups panko
vegetable oil for deep-frying

FOR THE MISO MAYO

150ml/5fl oz/scant ²⁄₃ cup Mayonnaise (page 32)
2 tbsp freshly squeezed lemon juice
2 tbsp light miso paste
1 tsp Sriracha sauce (see page 117)

FOR THE GARNISHES

1 unripe papaya or mango, julienned
a handful of chopped fresh coriander
a few spring onions, sliced
Sriracha sauce (page 117)

1. Mix together all the ingredients for the miso mayo and put to one side.
2. When eating-time is approaching, peel the prawns and put to one side. Mix together flour and salt on a tray, the beaten egg together with the milk on a second and the panko on a third. Heat a couple of centimetres of cooking oil in a pan with high edges to about 180°C/350°F (or until a bit of panko is sizzling nicely). Dip the prawns in the spiced flour first, then in the egg mixture and finally in the panko. Add them to the hot oil. Deep-fry quickly on both sides until the panko has turned a nice colour, then lift out with a slotted spoon and leave to drain on a piece of kitchen paper.
3. Assemble the bao by spreading some miso mayo on a slice of bread, add papaya, coriander and spring onion. Finish off with some Sriracha sauce.

HOME-MADE CHILLI SAUCE

To make your own chilli sauce is an art form and a lifelong project. Here follows a basic recipe that can be used just as it is or as a base for your own experiments. Vary by using different types of chilli or vinegar, whether you mix in garlic and other spices and for how long you leave it to ferment.

500g/1lb 2oz chillis of your choice
2 tbsp salt
350ml/12fl oz/1½ cups distilled vinegar, 6%

Blend together chilli and salt to a coarse purée. Transfer to a jar, put the lid on and leave to stand at room temperature for 24 hours so it just starts to ferment a little.

Add the 6% distilled vinegar. If you only have 12%, dilute it 50/50 with water. Leave at room temperature for 1–7 days. Check the seasoning from time to time and decide for yourself when it tastes funky enough. Blend everything together again and rub through a sieve to get rid of any peel and seeds. Pour into a nice bottle. Shake before use. It will keep for at least 3 months in the fridge.

Brioche

Offering this bread to a French baker and calling it brioche would probably make him or her start gasping for air, so don't do that. No, this is an Americanised version of the original buttery French breakfast bread, and this just happens to be perfect for sandwiches. It's soft and sweet with a little springiness. The light buttery crumb goes perfectly crispy when you heat it up in a frying pan. The same basic dough can be used for various shapes, and in this chapter we'll go through three of them: bun, hoagie and New England hot dog bun.

Brioche

Makes 8 buns

2 tsp fast-action dried
   yeast
250ml/9fl oz/generous
   1 cup tepid water
3 tbsp whole milk
2 eggs
540g/1lb 3oz/scant
   2 cups white strong
   bread flour, plus extra
   for dusting
2½ tbsp granulated sugar
1½ tsp salt
100g/3½oz butter, diced

1. Mix together the yeast, water and milk directly in the dough mixer bowl. Whisk one egg until fluffy and fold into the yeast mixture.
2. Mix together the flour, sugar and salt in a separate bowl. Add the butter and break it up into the flour. Add the flour mixture to the yeast mixture and knead in a mixer for 10 minutes or until the dough is smooth and nice, twice as long if you are kneading by hand. Shape into a ball, put it back in the bowl and leave to rise covered with clingfilm until the dough has doubled in size, about 2 hours.
3. Flour the backside of your hand and knock back the dough, pressing all the air out of it. Cover with clingfilm and leave to rise for 1 more hour.
4. Take out the dough and place on a floured worktop. Choose if you want to make buns, hoagies or New England hot dog buns, follow the instructions below and then cover the buns with a tea towel and leave to rise for 1 more hour.
5. Preheat the oven to 200°C/400°F/ gas 6. Place a large oven dish filled with water at the bottom of the oven. Beat the remaining egg together with a dash of water and brush the buns before you quickly and merrily shove them in the oven. Bake in the centre of the oven for 15–20 minutes, until the buns have turned a dark golden brown colour. Leave to cool.

BRIOCHE BUNS

The classic hamburger shape is easy to get right. Just divide the dough into eight equally sized parts, place a piece of dough in your cupped right hand and shape into a bun by folding the edges until a nice, tight bun shape appears.

HOAGIE

A hoagie is bigger and more rectangular than a round bun. To make the shape, you divide the dough into six parts, follow the instructions for the brioche buns but finish off by lightly rolling it out on a floured worktop.

NEW ENGLAND HOT DOG BUNS

Divide the dough into eight equally sized parts, roll them out to (very rough) triangles and fold the top and the bottom long side so they meet in the centre. Pinch together the seam and roll the dough into long cylinders, about the same length as a hot dog bun. Then place them on a normal oven tray with a 1cm/½in gap in between each bun or, if you can, in a New England hot dog bun pan. This to enable them to rise together into a batch but still be individual buns.

Brioche bun ———

Hoagie. ———

Torta de milanesa

Torta just means 'sandwich' in Mexican Spanish (tortilla means 'small sandwich'), while milanesa is the word for breaded fried meat. Together with beans, vegetables and some quick pickled cucumber, it will be a sandwich that's hard to forget.

Makes 4 sandwiches

4 Brioche Buns (page 128)
Crema (see page 132)
4 chicken breasts, about 150g/5oz each
60g/2¼oz/½ cup plain flour
2 tsp chilli powder
2 tsp cumin
1 tbsp ground paprika
1 tsp salt
1 egg
200g/7oz/2 cups panko
2 avocados, sliced
1 white onion, sliced
a bunch of fresh coriander
2–4 jalapeños
Quick Pickled Cucumber (see page 113)
vegetable oil for deep-frying
butter for frying

FOR REFRIED BEANS

400g/14oz can of black beans
3½ tbsp water
1 tsp dried epazote (optional)
olive oil for frying
salt and freshly ground black pepper

1. If the bread is baked and the crema from the fish taco torta recipe is done, you can start off by making the refried beans. It's simple. Just drain the liquid off a can of black beans and fry the beans in oil in a frying pan over a medium heat. After a while, you can add some water, and when the water has evaporated you mash the beans directly in the pan with a potato masher or similar. It should be creamy but chunky. Season with salt, pepper and, if you can get hold of it, epazote. It's a Mexican spice that tastes wonderful with beans and prevents wind.

2. Now it's nearly time for deep-frying! Butterfly the chicken breast by slicing it lengthways until nearly cut through and fold the meat out like a book. Bash it with a meat tenderiser or a pan or something until you get a 1cm/½in thick slice of chicken breast. If you want, you can cut it to better suit the sandwich shape. Heat the oil to around 160°C/325°F (or when a bit of panko is sizzling nicely). Mix together flour and spices on a plate, put the beaten egg on another and the panko on a third. Dip the chicken fillets in the spiced flour first, then in the egg and finally in the panko.

Deep-fry the chicken until golden and crispy. Leave to drain on a piece of kitchen paper.

3. Cut the brioche bun in half and fry in a little butter in a frying pan over a medium heat until it's coloured nicely. Assemble the sandwich by spreading refried beans on the bottom half, add some of the pickled cucumber followed by the fried chicken fillet. Finish off with sliced avocado, white onion and jalapeño, coriander and a mind-blowing amount of crema. Put the top brioche half on, shut up and eat.

Fish taco torta

If you don't like fish tacos, you don't like life. Or perhaps it's fish you don't like? Or tacos? I'm not quite sure. In any case the sandwich version of my favourite taco is just as tasty as the original. The tortilla crisps will give some nice extra crunch, but if you can't be bothered to fry your own it's fine to buy them.

Makes 8 buns

8 Brioche Buns (page 128)
Deli Coleslaw (page 55)
8 corn tortillas (or ready-made tortilla chips)
800g/1lb 12oz firm, white fish, such as cod
60g/2¼oz/½ cup plain flour
2 tsp chilli powder
2 tsp ground cumin
1 tbsp paprika
1 tsp salt
1 egg
100-150g/3½–5oz/ 2–3 cups panko
2 avocados, sliced
1 white onion, chopped
a bunch of fresh coriander, chopped
oil for deep-frying
butter for frying

FOR THE CREMA

4 garlic cloves
½ lime
100ml/3½fl oz/scant 1 cup Mayonnaise (page 32)
100g/3½oz/scant 1/3 cup crème fraîche
Sriracha (see page 117)

1. If the bread is baked and the slaw is done, you could perhaps start by making the crema, so that it's all done when it starts to get a bit busy further ahead. It's simple. Just crush the garlic and squeeze the lime and mix together with the other ingredients. Add chilli sauce to taste – but remember the crema is the only thing to contribute with spice in this dish, so don't be shy.

2. Now it's time to deep-fry! If you didn't buy ready-made tortilla crisps, cut the tortilla bread in quarters, heat the oil to 180°C/350°F (or try adding a piece of tortilla; if it sizzles nicely when added to the oil it's hot enough). Deep-fry the tortillas until golden and crispy. Leave to drain on kitchen paper. Sprinkle with salt.

3. Lower the heat of the oil to about 160°C/325°F. Cut the fish into sandwich-sized pieces. Mix together the flour and spices on a plate, the beaten egg on another and the panko on a third. Dip the fish in the spiced flour first, then in the egg and finally in the panko. Deep-fry for a couple of minutes on each side until the panko has coloured nicely, then leave to drain on a piece of kitchen paper.

4. Cut the brioche bun in half and fry in a little butter in a frying pan over a medium heat until it's coloured nicely. Assemble the sandwich by placing four tortilla crisps on the bottom half, then the slaw followed by the fried fish. Finish off with sliced avocado, chopped white onion and coriander as well as obscene amounts of crema. Put the lid on top and shove the whole lot into your pie hole.

Lobster roll

Lobster rolls have in recent years gone from a local American East Coast delicacy to something found countrywide. Therefore, a lot of different subspecies of this actually very simple sandwich have started to pop up. An authentic lobster roll only tastes of perfectly boiled lobster, butter, mayo, bread and maybe a pinch of old bay seasoning. Nothing else.

Serves 4

4 New England Hot Dog Buns (see page 128)

4 live lobsters

1 brown onion, halved

2 tbsp sea salt

4 garlic cloves

3 bay leaves

1 tsp black peppercorns

55g/2oz butter

4 garlic cloves

2 tbsp mayonnaise

freshly squeezed lemon juice

FOR THE OLD BAY SEASONING

1 tbsp celery salt

1 tbsp finely ground bay leaves

2 tsp freshly ground black pepper

1 tsp paprika

½ tsp mustard powder

1. If you want to be nice, you can render the lobster unconscious by placing it in the freezer for 2 hours before cooking. Then, push the tip of a large, heavy, sharp knife through the centre of the cross on its head (although many people cut out this step and just put the lobster head first into the boiling water). Bring a large pan of water to the boil. Add the onion, salt, garlic, bay leaves and black peppercorns, then add the lobster, head first. Take one or two at the time so that the water doesn't cool down. Boil until the shell has turned red, which normally means 6 minutes for a 500g/1lb 2oz large lobster and 10 minutes for one double that size. At this time they will be just a little underdone, which is the point.

2. Leave the lobsters to cool before de-shelling them. Place them in a bowl so you catch all the good meat juices, and break apart claws and tail and take out all the good meat. Remove the intestine. Use the blunt edge of a knife to crack the shells with if you've caught a tough one. Slice the lobster meat coarsely and add back to the juices.

3. The classic spice for lobster rolls is called old bay seasoning, but since you only can get hold of it in New England we'll have to make our own. Crush all the ingredients together into a fine powder using a pestle and mortar.

3. Bring a pan to medium heat. Add the butter and grate over the garlic. Hot dog buns of New England style are called top loaders, you cut them in half across the top instead of the side as in other countries, and the practical thing with this is that you can fry the sides so they get all crispy and garlicky. So do that.

4. Lower the heat and add the lobster to the butter. It should just warm through a little, so be careful so it doesn't get tough and dull. Place the lobster in a bowl, add the mayo and stir. Put the mixture in a hot dog bun, sprinkle over some old bay seasoning and serve as quick as a flash.

Meatball hero.

Meatball hero

Submarine is the correct name for this, but in Philadelphia it's called a hoagie, in New England a grinder and in New York a hero. The name was coined in the 1930s when it was claimed that only a true hero could eat such an enormous sandwich.

Makes 6 sandwiches

6 Hoagies (see page 128)
a few handfuls of rocket
3 balls of mozzarella

FOR THE SAUCE

1 onion, finely chopped
2 garlic cloves, chopped
400g/14oz can of whole tomatoes
½ tbsp tomato purée
1 tsp dried oregano
½ tsp chilli flakes
½ tsp granulated sugar
salt and black pepper
vegetable oil for frying

FOR THE MEATBALLS

½ onion
1 garlic clove
200g/7oz minced beef
200g/7oz minced pork
1 large egg
40g/1½oz/½ cup grated Parmesan cheese
1 tsp fennel seeds
a bunch of flat-leaf parsley
100ml/3½fl oz/scant ½ cup whole milk
50g/1¾oz/1 cup fresh breadcrumbs
olive oil for frying
salt and black pepper

1. Fry the onion and garlic for the tomato sauce in a little oil until soft. Add the tomatoes, tomato purée, oregano, chilli flakes and sugar. Mash up a little with a wooden spoon. Add the bay leaf, turn the heat down and leave to simmer gently while you get cracking on the meatballs. Season to taste with salt and black pepper.

2. Finely chop even more onion and garlic for the meatballs and fry them until soft in yet another bit of oil. Place the mince in a bowl, crack in the egg, add the onion, Parmesan, fennel seeds, finely chopped parsley (and any other herbs you might have at home), milk and breadcrumbs and mash everything together with your hands. Add salt and pepper.

3. Roll into meatballs about golf-ball size and fry them in oil in a cast-iron pan until seared. Fry off a small one that you've flattened out and taste. Nice? If not, add more salt and pepper. Then add the meatballs to the pan with the tomato sauce and leave to simmer for at least 1 hour. This way the meatballs will flavour the sauce and vice versa.

4. Preheat the oven to 200°C/400°F/gas 6. Halve the bread and fry the insides crispy in a pan with a little butter. Add a layer of rocket on the bottom half and then a couple of meatballs without too much sauce on them. Top with mozzarella and whack in the oven and bake until the cheese has melted. Pour over some sauce, put the lid on and squeeze. Voilà! The meatballs and the sauce also make a mean sauce for spaghetti.

OTHER COMMON NAMES FOR THE HERO SANDWICH

NEW JERSEY
Blimpie or Torpedo

ILLINOIS
Gondola

QUEBEC
Sous-marin

BOSTON
Spuckie

NEW ENGLAND
Tunnel

YONKERS
Wedge

PENNSYLVANIA
Zeppelin

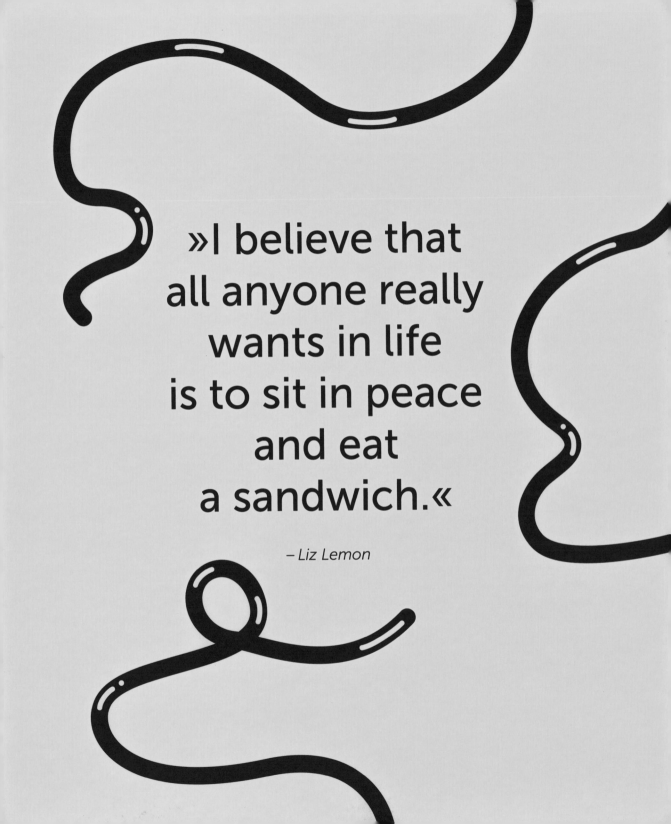

»I believe that
all anyone really
wants in life
is to sit in peace
and eat
a sandwich.«

– Liz Lemon

Porchetta sandwich

If you were to describe porchetta to someone who hasn't even seen this Italian delicacy you could say that it's a rolled-up pig, covered in its own crispy fried skin – like a kind of sausage for people who can't face the grinding. When you describe it like that I guess it doesn't sound especially appetising, but it is, and it becomes even tastier if served in a sandwich, of course.

Makes 8 sandwiches

8 brioche buns (see
    page 128)
butter
rocket

FOR THE PORCHETTA

2–3kg/4lb 8oz–6lb 8oz
    pork belly with rind
3 tbsp fennel seeds
2 tbsp chilli flakes
2 tbsp finely chopped
    fresh sage
1 tbsp finely chopped
    fresh rosemary
3 garlic cloves
salt

FOR THE SALSA VERDE

a bunch of fresh parsley
100ml/3½fl oz/scant
    ½ cup olive oil
2 tbsp fennel seeds
2 tsp coriander seeds
2 tsp chilli flakes
2 garlic cloves
finely grated zest of
    1 lemon
salt

1. Cut off the sinews, gristle and uneven bits from the pork belly so that you end up with a completely square, evenly thick bit of pork. Since crackling that isn't crispy is pretty horrid, you then make a mock porchetta by rolling it up as tight as you possibly can and mark where the rind will be overlapping itself. Roll out the meat again, cut off the excess bit of rind (keeping the meat of course) and, for a maximum crispy result, leave the meat to dry in the fridge for as long as you've time to wait for – up to 2 days works fine.

2. Before cooking, take out the pork belly and leave at room temperature for 1–2 hours. Score the rind making a nice criss-cross pattern and rub in a generous amount of salt. Toast the fennel seeds in a dry frying pan, then crush together with chilli flakes, sage, rosemary and finely chopped garlic using a pestle and mortar. Roll the porchetta up the same way as you practised in step 1 and tie together with cooking string.

3. Preheat the oven to 250°C/425°F/gas 7, then roast the porchetta for 40 minutes. Lower the heat to 150°C/300°F/gas 2 and keep cooking it until the inside temperature has reached 63°C/145°F, about another 1½–2 hours. If the crackling isn't crisping up nicely, turn the oven to max and cook for another 10 minutes, or alternatively, take out the porchetta and leave it to cool.

4. Combine all the ingredients for the salsa verde, seasoning to taste with salt and freshly squeezed lemon juice.

5. Assemble the sandwiches by cutting the buns in half and frying them in a little butter in a frying pan over medium heat until they get a bit of colour and turn crispy. Add a layer of rocket, a layer of sliced porchetta (don't forget the crispy crackling!) and to finish off, a little salsa verde. Stop quibbling and dig in!

Italian beef

Chicago's signature sandwich is simply called Italian beef and appeared when poor Italian workers bought the toughest and cheapest cuts of beef, slow cooked it and put it in a bun. The Italian beef is served either with cheese or with giardiniera (see page 105), dry or, as this one, wet. That is, with gravy on the side for dipping. It also comes as soaked, but it's nigh on impossible to eat that.

Serves 4

4 Hoagies (see page 128)
about 1kg/2lb 4oz beef
    chuck steak
1 brown onion, sliced
3 garlic cloves, finely
    chopped
100ml/3½fl oz/scant ½
    cup Japanese soy sauce
100ml/3½fl oz/scant
    ½ cup sherry
about 500ml/17fl oz/
    generous 2 cups water
1 fresh rosemary sprig
a bunch of fresh thyme
Mozzarella (see page 72)
    or provolone cheese
Dijon mustard
butter for frying
salt and freshly ground
    black pepper

FOR THE GRAVY

3 pieces of bone marrow
3 shallots
butter
500ml/17fl oz/generous
    2 cups beef stock
salt and freshly ground
    black pepper

1. Fry the onion in butter in a pan, add the garlic and place the meat on top. Add the soy sauce, sherry and water. Throw in some rosemary and thyme and season to taste with salt and pepper. Cover and leave to simmer until the meat is falling apart nicely, about 4 hours. Take out the meat and strain the beef stock.

2. Make your dipping sauce by roasting the bone marrow in the centre of the oven at 200°C/400°F/gas 6 for about 20 minutes. Finely chop the shallots and fry in butter until transparent in a frying pan over a medium heat. Add the beef stock and leave to simmer gently until reduced to half. Season to taste with salt and black pepper. Spoon out the marrow from the bones and add to the sauce.

3. Cut the buns in half and fry the insides until crispy in a little butter in a frying pan over a medium heat. Add a good amount of meat and a couple of slices of good-quality cheese. Serve with mustard and a bowl of bone marrow gravy on the side for dipping the sandwich in.

LITTLE ITALIAN BEEF
GLOSSARY

If you are going to Chicago you'll need to know how to properly order your Italian beef. Here follows a quick reference guide.

HOT DIPPED
The bread is dipped in gravy and served with meat and giardiniera.

HOT DIPPED COMBO
The bread is dipped in gravy and served with meat, giardiniera and sausage.

SWEET DRY
Dry bread with meat and topped with fried peppers.

GRAVY BREAD
The bread is dipped in gravy and served with giardiniera but without meat.

CHEESY BEEF
The bread is dipped in gravy and served with meat topped with cheese.

CHEESY BEEF ON GARLIC
The bread is prepared as garlic bread and served with meat topped with cheese.

Cream cheesesteak

The cheesesteak was invented in the 1930s by the sausage salesmen Pat and Harry Olivieri, who were messing about one day putting chopped meat and fried onion in a hot dog bun. A taxi driver sampled the creation and burst out that they should immediately stop selling sausage and instead go for this new fantastic sandwich. Today the cheesesteak is perhaps Philadelphia's number one tourist attraction, and as with all other iconic dishes there are a thousand different ways to prepare it. This is how I do it.

Makes 4 sandwiches

4 Hoagies (see page 128)
400g/14oz rib eye steak
Dijon or yellow mustard
    (see page 31)
8 slices of provolone
    cheese
1 ball of Mozzarella (see
    page 72)
olive oil and butter for
    frying
salt and freshly ground
    black pepper

FOR THE
PEPERONATA

3 garlic cloves
3 jalapeños
3 brown onion
3 pointed peppers
2 tbsp olive oil
3½ tbsp water
1½ tbsp red wine vinegar
salt and freshly ground
    black pepper

1. Ask your butcher to finely slice the rib eye or prepare it yourself by leaving the meat in the freezer for about 1 hour and then slice super-thinly.

2. Then get started on the peperonata, which is an Italian pepper and onion relish and perfect for cream cheese steaks. Finely chop the garlic, slice the jalapeño and slice onion and pepper into 1 cm thick slices. Fry them in oil in a frying pan on a medium heat for 5 minutes, add the water and lower the heat. Leave to simmer gently for about 40 minutes, until the vegetables have softened. Season to taste with vinegar, salt and pepper.

3. Heat up the oil and fry the rib eye in batches in a hot frying pan until crispy and nice. Season to taste with salt and pepper.

4. Cut the hoagie in half and fry the insides in a little butter until crispy. Spread with mustard. Now it's time to play diner chef: Lower the pan to a medium heat, divide the meat into 4 equally sized piles and shape them so they will fit your hoagie rolls.

Then place grated mozzarella and provolone on top of your meat, cover the frying pan with a lid and wait for a minute or so, until the cheese has melted. Add the hoagie-shaped meat to your buns, top with peperonata and the top half of the bread.

OTHER FAMOUS
CHEESESTEAKS

CHICKEN CHEESESTEAKS
Replace the beef with chicken.

PIZZA STEAK
Replace the peperonata with tomato sauce and even more mozzarella.

CHEESESTEAK HOAGIE
Replace the peperonata with sliced tomato and shredded iceberg lettuce.

Classic medianoche

A cubano, or Cuban sandwich, is essentially a simple pressed cheese and ham sandwich that was first popularised among Cuban immigrants in Miami's working class neighbourhood at the end of the nineteenth century. Mostly, the sandwich is made from a baguette, but if you instead, like here, use an eggier bread it's called a medianoche — which means midnight. And yes, this is the ultimate midnight snack.

Makes 6 sandwiches

6 Brioche Buns or Hoagies
    (see page 128)
Swiss cheese, such as
    Appenzeller or Comté
12 slices of smoked ham
Mayonnaise (see page 32)
Dill Pickles (see page 113)

FOR THE CARNITAS

1kg/2lb 4oz pork collar
200g/7oz lard (or oil)
1.5 litres/2½ pints/
    6½ cups water
1 tbsp salt

1. Good carnitas should be a great combination of textures, from thready to firm via crispy. This is how to make it. Dice the pork collar and bring to the boil together with lard, water and salt in a cast-iron pan. Lower the heat to medium and simmer gently, covered with a lid, for 45 minutes. Remove the lid and continue to simmer until all the water has evaporated, at which time the meat starts to fry crispy in the fat. When it's at its crispiest but before it's starting to become dry, remove from the heat.

2. Cut the buns in half and put a couple of slices of cheese on each half. Continue with smoked ham, a handful of carnitas, mayo and dill pickles. Put the halves together and place in a medium hot pan with a little butter, A cubano is a pressed sandwich, so some kind of weight is needed to press the sandwich down so it gets flat, crispy and melted cheesy. Turn over and fry for a little longer, about 4 minutes per side. Cut in half and serve immediately.

CHIMICHURRI

This originally Argentinean salsa is nowadays eaten throughout South America, and the world, and doesn't only go perfectly together with grilled meat. It's pretty damn fine to dip your sandwich in too.

a bunch of fresh parsley, chopped
3 garlic cloves, chopped
1 tbsp chopped fresh oregano,
    stalks removed
100ml/3½fl oz/scant
    ½ cup olive oil
2 tbsp red wine vinegar
½ tsp chilli flakes
salt and freshly ground
    black pepper

Mix together the parsley, garlic and oregano. Stir in the oil, vinegar and chilli flakes. Season to taste with salt and pepper.

Pork belly medianoche

If you'd like a chewier medianoche you can, as I've said, use a crispy banh mi baguette instead. Or you can follow this recipe and fill it with some thinly sliced and gloriously crispy pork belly instead. To ensure getting the balance right on your creation, make sure not to be stingy with either chilli sauce or mustard. Serve with some deep-fried plantain and a beer for maximum impact.

Makes 6 sandwiches

6 Brioche Buns or Hoagies (see page 128)
about 2kg/4lb 8oz pork belly
3½ tbsp salt
3½ tbsp granulated sugar
Swiss cheese, such as Appenzeller or Comté
Mustard (see page 31)
Mayonnaise (see page 32)
chilli sauce, such as Cholula
Deep-fried Plantains (see page 150)

1. Start the preparations one day ahead. Remove the rind from the pork belly and trim off the meat from where the ribs were attached so you get a neat and completely square bit of pork. Pat equal amounts of salt and sugar into the meat, wrap clingfilm around the meat and leave to dry cure in the fridge overnight.
2. The next day, preheat the oven to 220C/425°F/gas 7. Rinse all the salt off the meat, place it in an oven dish and roast in the centre of the oven for about 1 hour. Lower the heat to 120°C/250°F/gas ½ and leave to roast for another 1¼ hours. Take out the pork belly, try a little bit and then leave to cool completely so that you can cut it into nice slices.
3. Cut the buns in half and add a couple of slices of cheese to each half. Continue with sliced pork belly, then mustard, mayo and chilli sauce. Put the bread halves together, place them in a frying pan over a medium heat and press them as hard as you can. Cut in half and serve with deep-fried plantains.

HOW TO MAKE A DIRT-CHEAP SANDWICH PRESS

If you haven't got a luxurious sandwich press, you can do like some of the cubano places in Miami and create the world's simplest and cheapest grill press. Just wrap a brick in a double layer of kitchen foil and then press the hell out of the sandwich. A stylish and clever usage of a brick.

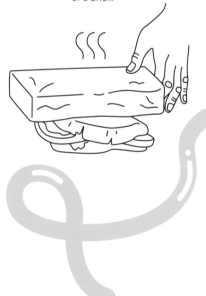

Chifles.

FROM SCRATCH: SIDES

Serves 2

1 plantain
vegetable oil for
   deep-frying
salt

CHIFLES These South American snacks are amazingly crispy and taste like something in between standard potato crisps and banana chips. If you can't get hold of plantain you can try green bananas – even though the flavour won't be quite the same.

1. Peel the plantains by cutting the skin in sections and then pick the pieces off. Cut into long, thin slices lengthways using a mandolin or a potato peeler. Heat the oil to 180°C/350°F and deep-fry the bananas for about 5 minutes until golden and crispy. Leave to drain on a piece of kitchen paper. Sprinkle with salt. Eat immediately. They're also perfect for putting in a burger instead of the potatoes in the Frita recipe (see page 154).

---

about 500g/1lb 2oz pork
   rind
1½ tsp salt
1 tsp brown sugar
1 tsp ground chilli
vegetable oil for
   deep-frying

CHICHARONES What do you do with the rind when you've made a dish using pork belly – that's right, chicharones, South American super-crispy deep-fried pork rind. Perfect as a snack or in sandwiches for extra crunch.

1. Place the pork rind in a pan and just cover with water, then simmer gently for 2 hours. Take it out carefully and leave to cool in the fridge for about 2 hours, until completely cold. Scrape off as much of the remaining fat from the underside of the rind as you can. Put the rind on a rack in the centre of the oven with a tray underneath. Set to the lowest possible heat and leave the skin to dry, with the oven door open, for about 8 hours.
2. Cut, or break, the dried rind into bite-sized pieces. Heat the oil to 180°C/350°F and deep-fry the rinds until they bubble up and become super-crispy. Leave to drain on a piece of kitchen paper. Mix together the spices and sprinkle on top.

FROM SCRATCH: SIDES

Serves 2

2 Dill Pickles (see
  page 113)
3½ tbsp plain flour
100g/3½oz/ cornflour
100ml/3½fl oz/scant
  ½ cup buttermilk
vegetable oil for
  deep-frying

FRIED DILL PICKLES **When choosing condiments for your sandwich you can go two ways: pickled or fried. However, this ingenious side dish combines the two, and you get both crispiness and delicious sweet-sour.**

1. Slice the gherkins and leave them to dry on a piece of kitchen paper. Mix together the flours in a bowl and pour the buttermilk in another. Heat the oil to 180°C/350°F and dip the gherkin slices firstly in the buttermilk, then in the flour, then deep-fry until crispy and golden. Leave to drain on a piece of kitchen paper.

500g/1lb 2oz baking
  potatoes
2 garlic cloves, unpeeled
1 tbsp plain flour
1 tsp salt
40g/1½oz/½ cup grated
  Parmesan cheese
vegetable oil for frying

TATER TOTS **For a long time, junk food nerds have discussed how to really get a perfectly creamy inner and a super-crispy outer on your fries. The answer: you make tater tots instead.**

1. Preheat the oven to 220°C/425°F/gas 7. Bake the potatoes and garlic in the centre of the oven for about 40 minutes until they've softened. Leave to cool and then peel the potato and grate it coarsely. Mix together with the rest of the ingredients, press out the roasted garlic from its skin and mush everything together to a compact mash.
2. Form the potatoes into small tubes – think mini fizzy drink cans – heat the oil to 180°C/350°F and deep-fry them, two at a time, for about 5 minutes until golden brown and crispy. Leave to drain on a piece of kitchen paper. Season to taste with salt and eat.

Fried dill pickles. ─────

Frita

South Florida's sandwich culture is almost completely defined by its vicinity to Cuba. And if the cubano is a South American version of the Italian pressed sandwich, the frita is the southern answer to the hamburger. But instead of eating the fries on the side, you put them in the burger. If you want to be properly authentic you drink a glass of batido de trigo with it (recipe below).

Makes 6 sandwiches

6 Brioche Buns (see
    page 128)
6 floury potatoes
Cuban Ketchup (see
    page 28)
6 fresh chorizo sausages
500g/1lb 2oz mince from
    beef chuck steak
2 white onions, sliced
vegetable oil for
    deep-frying
butter for frying
salt and freshly ground
    black pepper

1. Heat the oil to 180°C/350°F. Julienne the potato finely (see page 84) and deep-fry quickly until crispy and nice. Leave to drain on a piece of kitchen paper. Sprinkle with salt. Prepare the ketchup, if you haven't done so already.
2. Remove the skin from the fresh, preferably super-hot, chorizo sausages and mix the sausage meat together with the beef mince. Add salt and pepper if needed. Shape into balls and heat a cast-iron pan to as hot as you can. Place the balls in the pan and press out, using a broad spatula or grill press, to a burger with a lovely crispy edge. Fry until crispy.
3. Cut the buns in half and fry the insides in a little butter until crispy over a medium heat. Place the onion on the bottom half, then ketchup, meat patty, a pile of newly fried shoestring potato and finally the top half of the bun. Dig in.

BATIDO DE TRIGO

Cuban milkshakes often contains puffed wheat and tastes, by pure coincidence, exactly like those last wonderful drips of milk left in the bowl once you'd eaten the sugary breakfast puffs when little. Flashback warning issued.

MAKES 2 GLASSES

400ml/14fl oz/1¾ cups whole milk
3 tbsp sweetened condensed milk
100ml/3½fl oz/
scant ½ cup crushed ice
1 cup sweetened puffed
wheat cereal
a pinch of salt

Mix together all the ingredients and drink immediately.

Ice-cream
SANDWICHES

You didn't think I was going to write a whole book about sandwiches and not include a few recipes for ice-cream sandwiches, did you? To put a scoop of home-made ice cream in between home-made cookies and then squeeze together is one of the finest moments in life.

Klondike sandwich

There are plenty of different versions of this sandwich, so why should you then make a home-made Klondike sandwich when there are so many other versions you can buy? Well, I don't know. Why do you do anything at all? The answer is, because you feel like it, of course.

Makes 8 ice-cream sandwiches

VANILLA ICE CREAM

2 eggs
200g/7oz/1 cup granulated sugar
500ml/17fl oz/generous 2 cups whipping or double cream
250ml/9fl oz/generous 1 cup whole milk
2 tsp vanilla extract

FOR THE CHOCOLATE BISCUITS

300g/11oz butter, at room temperature
350g/12oz/1¾ cups granulated sugar
2 egg yolks
1 tbsp vanilla extract or 1 vanilla pod
360g/12¼oz/3 cups plain flour, plus extra for dusting
200g/7oz/2 cups cocoa powder
1 tsp salt

1. To make ice cream you will need, firstly, an ice-cream maker, and secondly, enough sense to look after it. If you have those two things, it only remains to get started. Start by whisking the eggs using an electric whisk until nice and fluffy. Mix in the sugar, a little at a time, so that everything dissolves. Stir in the cream, milk and vanilla extract and have a little taste. Nice, huh? Pour the ice-cream mixture into your ice-cream maker and run until it starts to look like soft scoop. Line a dish with greaseproof paper and pour in the ice cream. Make sure the dish is deep and large enough to make the ice cream 2–3 cm/¾–1¼in thick. This is because you'll cut it into ice-cream squares later to put in your sandwich. Put in the freezer.

2. Preheat the oven to 180°C/350°F/gas 4. Fit the paddle attachment onto your mixer or the whisk attachment to your hand-held mixer and beat the butter and sugar until fluffy, about 3 minutes. Add the egg yolks and vanilla extract and whisk for another 3 minutes. Mix together the flour, cocoa powder and salt and add this to the butter mixture. Mix until you get a dough. Wrap the cookie dough in some clingfilm and leave in the fridge for 1 hour.

3. Cut the dough in half and roll out one half to about 5mm/¼in thickness on a floured worktop. The other half you can either save in the fridge or bake off straight away. You decide.

4. Now to the fiddly bits. Cut the dough into equal squares in a size of your choice. Eat up the leftover bits. Carefully transfer the biscuits to a tray covered in baking parchment using a knife or something. Make some decorative holes using the tip of a retracted pen. Whack in the centre of the oven and bake for 10–15 minutes. The biscuits should be still be a bit soft, but not so soft that they fall apart.

5. Assemble the ice-cream sandwiches by turning the ice-cream tray upside-down, pull off the parchment and cut the ice cream into the same-sized squares as the biscuits. Sandwich the ice cream in between two biscuits and dig in.

Banana bread ice cream sandwich

Banana bread is, of course, nice to eat on its own or just with a cup of coffee. But it's also superb in an ice-cream sandwich. This banana cake, in particular, is baked in a deep oven tray instead of a loaf tin, which means it becomes a kind of dessert focaccia for bad-asses. For best flavour, choose bananas as ripe as possible.

Makes 8 ice-cream sandwiches

FOR THE RUM AND COCONUT ICE CREAM

2 eggs
200g/7oz/1 cup granulated sugar
2 tbsp dark rum
400ml/14fl oz/1¾ cups whipping or double cream
300ml/10½fl oz/generous 1¼ cups coconut milk

FOR THE BANANA BREAD

85g/3oz butter, at room temperature
250g/9oz/1¼ cups granulated sugar
1 egg
150ml/5fl oz/scant ⅔ cup buttermilk
2 tbsp olive oil
2 super-ripe bananas
250g/9oz/2 cups plain flour
¾ tsp bicarbonate of soda
½ tsp baking powder
½ tsp salt

1. Start by making the ice cream. Whisk the eggs until fluffy using an electric whisk. Mix in the sugar, a little at a time. Pour in the rum, cream and coconut milk. Leave in the fridge while you prepare your ice-cream machine. Follow the instructions for whichever model you have and then churn the ice cream like the wind, old friend. When it has the same consistency as soft scoop, line a baking tin or mould with baking parchment and pour in the ice cream. Remember that the form needs to be deep and large enough so to make the ice cream about 4cm/1½in thick. This because you will cut the ice cream into squares to put in your sandwich. Put in the freezer.

2. Now it's time to bake the cake. Preheat the oven to 180°C/350°F/gas 4. Fit the paddle attachment onto your mixer or the whisk attachment to your hand-held mixer and beat the butter and sugar until fluffy, about 3 minutes. Add an egg and whisk for another 3 minutes. Add the buttermilk and oil, increase the speed and whisk until the batter is completely white, about 5–6 minutes more. Meanwhile you can mash the bananas and mix together the flour, bicarbonate of soda, baking powder and salt. Lower the speed, add the bananas and then the flour mixture. Line the bottom of a deep oven tray with baking parchment, pour in the batter and whack it in the oven, centre shelf. Bake until a skewer comes up dry when inserted, about 30 minutes. Leave to cool.

3. Cut a portion-sized piece of the banana bread, cut it in half and grill it so the top gets crispy. If you have an outdoor grill you use that of course, if not a griddle or even a non-stick pan will do the trick. Turn the ice cream upside-down, remove the paper and cut into squares same size as you've cut the banana bread. Sandwich the square ice cream in between two pieces of banana bread and dig in.

Cop coffee ice-cream sandwich

A black coffee and a doughnut is a real classic in police circles but actually not that practical, as you could spill the hot coffee all over your lap during car chases. A better alternative is to make the whole thing into an ice-cream sandwich. Then you can enjoy your snack and keep one hand free for chasing bad guys.

Makes 10–12

DOUGHNUTS

250ml/9fl oz/generous
   1 cup whole milk
3½ tbsp granulated sugar
2 tsp dried yeast
155g/2oz butter
2 eggs
540g/1lb 3oz/4¾ cups
   plain flour, plus extra for
   dusting
½ tsp salt
vegetable oil for deep-
   frying and greasing

COFFEE ICE CREAM

2 eggs
200g/7oz/1 cup
   granulated sugar
500ml/17fl oz/generous
   2 cups whipping or
   double cream
250ml/9fl oz/generous
   1 cup whole milk
2 tsp instant coffee

COFFEE ICING

6 tbsp icing sugar
2 tsp instant coffee
2 tsp water

1. Start by making doughnuts. Warm the milk until tepid. Add the sugar and dried yeast. Melt the butter and leave to cool a little, add the eggs and whisk until combined. Stir in the yeast mixture, then flour and salt and let the dough mixer knead the dough for 10 minutes, double the time if you are using your hands. Shape into a ball on a lightly floured worktop, place in a greased tin, cover with clingfilm and leave in the fridge for at least 8 hours, preferably overnight.

2. Once the dough has finished cold rising, roll it out on a floured worktop until about 2cm/¾in thick. Using a glass or a cutter, cut out doughnut-sized circles and then, with some little round thing, cut out the holes. These you can save and make into doughnut holes. They're good. Leave your doughnuts to rise at room temperature for 1½ hours or until they look nice and fluffy. Heat the deep-frying oil to 180°C/350°F and deep-fry a couple of doughnuts at a time until the bottom side has coloured beautifully, then flip them over and fry the other side as well. Leave to drain on kitchen paper.

3. Let's do the ice cream, shall we? Whisk the eggs with an electric whisk until fluffy. Mix in the sugar, a little at a time. Pour in the cream, milk and instant coffee. Leave in the fridge for at least 1 hour. Follow the instructions for your ice-cream machine and churn the ice cream. When it has the consistency of soft scoop, place a piece of greaseproof paper in a tin and pour in the ice cream. Remember that the tin should be as large and deep enough to make the ice cream about 4cm/1½in thick because you will cut out ice-cream circles to put in your sandwich. Put in the freezer.

4. Make the coffee icing by stirring together the icing sugar, instant coffee and water into a shiny sauce. Dip the tip of your doughnut and leave to set for a minute. Cut your doughnuts in half. Turn the ice cream upside-down, remove the paper and cut out ice-cream circles using a glass or a cutter or something. The only important thing is to make them roughly the same size as your doughnuts. Sandwich the ice cream in between the doughnut halves and go downtown to solve some crimes.

Old-fashioned ice-cream sandwich

Don Draper does already look very handsome with an Old-fashioned in his hand, but imagine how much cooler he'd have been with an ice-cream sandwich in his hand instead! This ice-cream sandwich comes with the flavours of the classic cocktail. A blondie is, if you were wondering, a paler version of a brownie.

Makes 8

3 tbsp maraschino
   cherries

ANGOSTURA ICE CREAM

2 eggs
200g/7oz/1 cup
   granulated sugar
500ml/17fl oz/generous
   2 cups whipping cream
250ml/9fl oz/generous
   1 cup whole milk
2 tsp vanilla extract or
   1 vanilla pod
20 dashes of angostura
   bitters

BOURBON BLONDIES

225g/8oz butter, at
   room temperature
400g/14oz/2 cups light
   soft brown sugar
2 eggs
300g/11oz/1¾ cups plain
   flour
1 tsp bicarbonate of soda
½ tsp salt
1 tbsp vanilla extract or
   1 vanilla pod
2 tbsp bourbon
1 orange

1. Start with the ice cream. Whisk the eggs with an electric whisk until nice and fluffy. Mix in the sugar, a little at a time, until everything is dissolved. Stir in the cream, milk and vanilla extract and dash in the angostura bitters. Taste. Yum. Pour the ice-cream mixture in your ice-cream machine and run until it starts to look like soft scoop. Pour in a tin and place in the freezer.

2. Preheat the oven to 180°C/350°F/gas 4. Fit the paddle attachment to your mixer or the whisk to your hand-held mixer and beat butter and sugar until fluffy, about 3 minutes. Add the eggs and whisk for another 3 minutes. Mix together the flour, bicarbonate of soda and salt, and add the vanilla and bourbon. Grate in the orange zest. Have a taste of this wonderful batter. Line a deep tin with greaseproof paper, pour over the batter and whack in the oven. Bake until the batter doesn't wobble any more, 25–30 minutes. Leave to cool. Cut your blondies into squares, add a scoop of angostura ice cream and a spoonful of maraschino cherries, preferably of the brand Luxardo. Finish off with another blondie.

HOW TO MAKE AN OLD-FASHIONED COCKTAIL

This classic cocktail from 1806 is one of those proper, er, cocktails! Of course, you'll need to know how to make a mean version of it. This was originally drunk as a morning cocktail, so no whinging about it being strong, okay?

MAKES 1 COCKTAIL

1 Demerara sugar cube
3 dashes of angostura bitters
1 dash of water
3½ tbsp bourbon or rye
2 pieces of orange peel
1 maraschino cherry

Place the sugar cube in a tumbler and dash with angostura bitters. Squeeze the oils out of a piece of orange peel, add a dash of water and muddle until the sugar has dissolved. Add bourbon and ice and stir until the glass gets frosty. Serve with an orange twist and a maraschino cherry.

165

Ice cream sandwiches

So simple, so nice. Here follows three varieties of ice-cream sandwiches that I happen to like. Use these recipes as a base for further experimentation.

Makes 6

FOR THE ICE CREAM

2 eggs
200g/7oz/1 cup granulated sugar
500ml/17fl oz/generous 2 cups whipping cream
250ml/9fl oz/generous 1 cup whole milk

FOR THE COOKIES

110g/3½oz butter, at room temperature
3½ tbsp granulated sugar
100g/3½oz/½ cup brown sugar
1 egg
½ tsp vanilla extract or ½ vanilla pod
150g/5oz/1¼ cups plain flour
½ tsp salt
½ tsp baking powder

FOR PISTACHIO

100g/3½oz/¾ cup pistachio nuts
white chocolate

FOR CHOCOLATE

100g/3½oz dark chocolate
100g/3½oz pretzels
pecans

FOR VANILLA

2 tsp vanilla extract or 1 vanilla pod
2 vanilla wafers
macadamia nuts

1. Start by making the ice cream. Whisk the eggs with an electric whisk until fluffy. Mix in the sugar, a little at a time. For pistachio ice cream: grind the pistachios into a fine powder and add after you've added milk and cream. For the chocolate ice cream: melt the chocolate with the milk and mix together with the cream. For the vanilla ice cream: add the milk, cream and vanilla extract. Leave in the fridge while preparing your ice-cream maker. Follow the instructions for your model. When the ice cream has the same consistency as soft scoop, you pour it in a tin and put in the freezer.

2. Now it's time to bake the cookies. Preheat the oven to 180°C/350°F/gas 4. Fit the paddle attachment to your mixer or the whisk to your hand-held mixer and beat the butter and sugar until fluffy, about 3 minutes. Add the egg and vanilla extract and whisk for another 3 minutes. Mix together the flour, baking powder and salt in a bowl and add to the butter mixture.

3. If you want to make pistachio ice-cream sandwiches, chop white chocolate and add to the dough. If you want to make the chocolate ice-cream sandwiches you do the same thing with pecan nuts, and for the vanilla ice-cream sandwiches, macadamia nuts. Leave the dough to cool in the fridge. Divide the dough in 12 and roll into balls. Place them on a baking tray lined with baking parchment and flatten out a little. Bake for 11–15 minutes. Leave to cool.

4. Prepare the topping by separately crushing pistachio nuts and pretzels coarsely. Blend the vanilla wafers into a fine powder. Assemble the sandwiches by placing a scoop of ice cream in between two cookies, squeeze together and then roll each cookie in its designated topping. Okay? See you later.

THE SANDWICH LOVER'S

New York

IN A FAKE news announcement on the satire site, *The Onion*, it was reported that Pew Research Center in Washington had found that Americans are world leaders in 'their ability to take very large sandwiches into their hands and crush them until they are small enough to fit inside the human mouth'. Everyone who's ever eaten a lunch sandwich in the USA knows, however, that there's nothing fake about that news piece at all. Americans really are incredibly skilled at eating sandwiches. While I'm sitting down to eat a pastrami on rye at what should be all sandwich-lovers' Ground Zero, New York's Lower East Side, I'm fascinated by the sizes of the sandwiches that the other guests successfully manage to squeeze into their mouths. I envy the ease with which they handle even the most unsteady of sandwich constructions and how they almost instinctively – as *The Onion* also reports – are 'sealing off the sides and back of the sandwich with a grip so powerful it completely eliminates the loss of any wayward pickles or tomatoes'. And it's not only **how** the Americans eat sandwiches that is fascinating but also what their sandwich culture says about them as people. Because Americans are incredibly proud of their sandwiches. They are are everywhere – from the simplest little hole-in-the-wall via nerdy sandwich blogs and enthusiastic newspaper articles to the menus of the most fancy of restaurants. But above all they are served in those really famous sandwich restaurants.

At the moment I'm sat at **Katz's Delicatessen**, for example – perhaps the most iconic of all of New York's Jewish delis. The restaurant was opened in 1888 by two Dutch immigrants, and here a huge number of TV cops have met their secret whistle-blowers, while it was at this exact table (that I've just managed to spill a whole load of pastrami on) that Meg Ryan faked an orgasm in *When Harry Met Sally*.

A couple of doors down lies the herring and sandwich shop **Russ & Daughters**, which was established in 1914 by the Polish immigrant Joel Russ and whose famous sandwich the Super Heebster is an incredibly beautiful creation, with its whitefish and bright green fly fish roe. And just a matzo ball's throw away, **2nd Ave Deli**, which, in contrast to a lot of other delis, actually serve their food kosher, even though the most orthodox Jews don't eat here as they stay open during the Sabbath.

The fact that all these restaurants are located just where they are is, however, not a coincidence. Until a couple of years ago, Lower East Side has always been a poor working class neighbourhood and the first stop for many of the city's immigrants. The food culture here has never been a matter of status and food nerdiness but about, as Joel Russ always used to say, 'parnosa'. About surviving. About making a living. About getting something cheap and filling for lunch. But also, of course, about getting a chance to catch your breath in an otherwise tough workday and for a little while enjoy a really damn good sandwich before it's time to get back to work.

The sandwiches were brought from home in lunch boxes or were bought wrapped in waxed paper. It was cheap, portable and filling food, whose practical bread wrap made it perfectly suitable to eat at a desk, in a building site office, or whilst sat on a piece of scaffolding 200 metres up in the air. The lunch sandwich was, and is, simply the gastronomy of the working men and women, and pretty much all of the classic American sandwiches were at some point invented to feed carpenters, welders and secretaries.

The proudness belonging to the working class is something that's always characterised the American people – perhaps because they once worked so hard to colonise the country. From the country music's somewhat smug lyrics, via the mythologised cowboy and settler to Bruce Springsteen's and the fold rock's romanticisation of factory workers, petty thieves and normal decent grafters. Yes, here in New York even the grafters have a certain vain swagger about them. They're walking down Second Avenue in their hard hats with their perfectly worn leather gloves hanging out from the back pockets of their Dickies and look like they were walking down Milan's Corso Como. So it's not that strange that workers' clothes are worn for fashion in other countries: from Levi's and Wrangler to Carhartt and Red Wings.

Not far from Lower East Side, in Little Italy, is **Parm** – a sandwich restaurant that could be used to illustrate the gentrification that the area has gone through during the last ten years. Parm, you see, is a modern take on all those Italian sandwich shops that used to feed the large Italian community in New York. Left today are, for example, the 112-year-old **Alleva** in Little Italy – which is also New York's oldest cheese shop. Just like its predecessors, Parm serves an Americanised processed-cheese-saturated version of Italian cuisine, both postmodernist-aware and proud to be a cultural junction. It's also the kind of restaurant that a lot of people wouldn't hesitate to put the epithet 'hipster' in front of.

To mock hipsters is not unusual nowadays, but I see this kind of youth culture only as something positive. Where the traditional restaurants often get stuck in a time when there wasn't anything dodgy about cheating with quality and using semi-prepared ingredients, young food artisans rediscover – like for example at the new and hip New York classic **Minetta Tavern** or the food hall **Gotham West Market** – the methods of old times, and prepare the food as it once was meant to be prepared: from scratch and using locally sourced, organic and carefully selected ingredients. Symptomatically enough, the hip **Mile End Deli** in Boerum Hill was also recently ranked New York's best deli by the restaurant guide *Zagat*, just ahead of said Katz's Delicatessen.

No, there's something about the widespread hipster contempt that's nothing more than a more politically correct version of hostility towards change. But 'the mixture is all of us and we're still mixing', as Woody Guthrie wrote back in the 1940s. Because if you want your culture to stay static, and preserved in amber, you can actually go and visit a museum. The sandwich culture is just like language, fashion, cities and our brains – in constant evolution – and even if there's not so much Italian and Eastern European immigration into the US right now, the increasingly large number of Latin American and Asian immigrants have already started to put their stamp on the city's sandwich offering. The **Momofuku** restaurant has transformed the Taiwanese gua bao into a worldwide matter, and both **Café Ollin's** Mexican tortillas and cemitas, as well as **Bánh Mì Zòn's** super-crispy Vietnamese banh mis have only turned New York into an even richer city.

Because apart from being able to 'crush them until they are small enough to fit inside the human mouth', it's just this wonderfully exciting kind of culture mash-up that Americans in general and New Yorkers in particular are world leaders in.

ADDRESSES

KATZ'S DELICATESSEN
205 East Houston Street
Pastrami on rye*

RUSS & DAUGHTERS
179 East Houston Street
The super heebster*

2ND AVENUE DELI
1442 First Avenue and
162 East 33rd Street
Corned beef sandwich*

PARM
248 Mulberry Street
Chicken parm hero*

DEFONTE'S
261 Third Avenue
The Nicky special*

ALLEVA
118 Grand Street
The meatball sub*

MINETTA TAVERN
113 MacDougal Street
French dip*

GOTHAM WEST MARKET
600 11th Avenue
Ship's biscuits at Little Chef*

MOMOFUKU SSÄM BAR
207 Second Avenue
Steamed buns*

CAFÉ OLLIN
339 East 108th Street
Juancho cemita*

BÁNH MÌ ZÒN
443 East 6th Street
Zon sandwich*

*EAT!

INDEX

**Are you on Instagram? Tag
your sandwich pictures with
#sandwichgram**

First published in Great Britain in 2015 by
Pavilion Books
1 Gower Street, London WC1E 6HD

www.pavilionbooks.com

This book can be ordered direct from the
publisher at www.pavilionbooks.com

Commisioning editor: Emily Preece-Morrison
Translator: Frida Green

ISBN: 978-1-909815-84-1

A CIP catalogue record for this book
is available from the British Library.

10 9 8 7 6 5 4 3 2 1

Reproduction by Mission Productions Ltd,
Hong Kong
Printed and bound by 1010 Printing
International Ltd, China

First published in Sweden in 2014 as *Mackor*
by Natur & Kultur, Stockholm
www.nok.se

© 2014 Jonas Cramby
Natur & Kultur, Stockholm
Photography: Roland Persson
Photographs pages 4, 168, 169, 170 and 173:
Jonas Cramby
Design and illustration: Kristin Lidström
Editor: Maria Nilsson